Praise for *Don't Think So Much*

"A comprehensive roadmap for pragmatic digital transformation, from Jim's own experience and success on that journey. *Don't Think So Much* has done what so many 'how to' books in this space fail to do – address the people and leadership component that is so critical to making digital change happen. His thoughtful approach to how to lead, how to inspire and how to teach innovation is sure to help you unleash the power of your people to get you to the future."

Diana Smith, business development leader
Sales & Marketing

"*Don't Think So Much* offers the reader a holistic overview on what Digitization in a business really means and where the challenges in going digital lie. The book demystifies the buzz around topics like IoT, Smart Products, and Industry 4.0, linking digital transformation with modern business practice in a simple and practicable way while considering the human aspect of it all."

Florian Pfefferle, industrial manufacturing executive
Operations

"Jim is that approachable CIO every company wishes they had leading them into the future. In *Don't Think So Much*, he deconstructs tech innovation, specifically corporate transformation through digital, in a way that is accessible and fun no matter what your role."

Laurie Swanson, talent development entrepreneur
Human Resources

D1160741

don't think so much

A Simpler Approach to Digital Transformation
that Creates Value and Connects People

James P. MacLennan

MT PRESS
CHICAGO

MT Press
Attn: Permissions
27 N. Wacker Drive, Ste 117
Chicago, IL 60606

... or contact us online at ...
www.dontthinksomuch.com
www.makerturtle.com

Published in the United States by MT Press,
an imprint of Maker Turtle LLC

ISBN: 978-1-951071-00-4 (e-Book)
ISBN: 978-1-951071-01-1 (Paperback)
ISBN: 978-1-951071-02-8 (Hardcover)

Library of Congress Control Number: 2019911859

Copyeditors: Catherine Driscoll and Marcia Dwyer
Cover Design: James P. MacLennan and Erin Roll
Interior Design: James P. MacLennan

Printing History:

August 2019   Version 1.0 (Loggerhead) - First Edition

I can call spirits from the vasty deep.

Why, so can I, or so can any man;
But will they come when you do call for them?

- William Shakespeare, King Henry IV, Part 1

Contents

About the Book

Updates

The digital world has changed the publishing industry in many ways; for example, it is much easier to make additions and improvements and get them distributed to the market. *Don't Think So Much* is updated as often as necessary. You are reading the Loggerhead version of this text; to see what has been added or updated since your book was printed, go to dontthinksomuch.com and check out the Updates link.

Hyperlinks

In the electronic version of the book, there are a number of hyperlinks to supporting information and other points of interest around the web. If you are reading the print version, I can save you some typing; go to dontthinksomuch.com and take a look at the Link Library.

Join the Conversation

We are only scratching the surface here! The *Field Notes* sections of this book are meant to illustrate ideas and concepts with real-world stories of digital transformation – and new stories are happening every day! Projects large and small, with varying levels of success. New approaches to drive change, manage people, and create engagement. And new connections to make, with people and organizations that are going through the same changes as the ones you are working through.

So visit dontthinksomuch.com and join the conversation! Come with questions – and be prepared to share your ideas!

Acknowledgments

This is a self-published work, and I did so for many reasons – not the least of which was an interest in the mechanics of the process and a long-time passion for the written word. That said – wow, what a humbling experience!

Major thanks go to my editors – Catherine Driscoll and Marcia Dwyer. I suppose the proud author would say that the edit process was tough, but I found it to be extremely enlightening – I did not realize how much I could improve my prose. I learned a lot; thank you very much C & M!

Catherine also helped tremendously through the entire publishing process. If you are looking for an accomplished editor that can also help with the self-publishing process, check out her work at Red Communications LLC.

Also thanks to Erin Roll for work on the final cover design. I got a lot of input on my ideas – but this was another process where it helped to have an experienced eye!

There are a lot of people that I have talked to about this project over the past year, too many to list out. Be assured, however, that your coaching, feedback, and encouragement has been heeded, and made its way into the finished product. Thanks for your patience with my questions, your generosity of ideas – and holding me accountable!

don't think
so much

Chapter 1

Being Digital in a Human World

We are truly living in a digital world – an environment enabled, driven, and dominated by bits and bytes, data and information, systems and technology. All this digital "stuff" has high-minded aspirations to enrich our lives with capability and convenience while creating economic growth and driving sustainable value.

In this environment, businesses are repeatedly encouraged to "embrace digital" and transform themselves to take advantage of exciting new developments in process and technology. Driven strongly by profound changes in capabilities and expectation, and manifested by exciting new products and services in consumer markets, this enticement to digital is tough to avoid.

To some extent, the Industrial economy has been able to resist these shiny new objects; value chains, market dynamics, and product complexities in the world of business-to-business commerce (B2B) have limited the application of fast-twitch, socially connected, fashion-driven demand for digital transformation. But changes in demographics, the expansion of mobile technologies, and the advent of the Internet of Things (aka Industrial Internet 4.0 or Smart, Connected Products) have closed the loop. These new ideas promise (or threaten) a fundamental transformation of products and services in the Industrial and B2B worlds.

Embracing the Change

"Being Digital" – thinking and acting with a truly digital mindset – is absolutely a participation sport. Over the years, businesses have practiced this sport by getting their hands dirty with the technology as it morphed and matured. And many aspects of this sport are still actively changing and maturing, as society incorporates new tools into our daily lives.

As an example, in our digital lifetimes we have seen Facebook progress through a fascinating life cycle, completing the arc from newcomer to must-have to has-been. Its text-based core has been replaced by the more visually engaging YouTube and Instagram. As a result, Facebook is now losing attention share with the younger demographic and its future is less certain.

Surprisingly, Digital Is Everywhere

Digital transformations occur every day in every corner of the world. I was reminded of this on a recent vacation to Africa – when you are off on safari, you truly are disconnected from the digital world. Forget about Wi-Fi in the safari camp. You are so far from civilization that telephone coverage is nonexistent. But I realized that technology is still not completely dependent on a live connection to the Internet. Using my notepad and voice recorder, I could work seamlessly with these simple tools.

Please believe me – I was happy to leave the always-connected lifestyle behind, and the expectation that I was connected and reachable 24x7. In my role as Chief Information Officer for a global, highly decentralized industrial corporation, I travel extensively to connect with and support people in IT, Finance, Operations, Sales, and Product Development functions. And because I work for a global company, some of my working locations can be quite interesting. A 10-day "cold turkey" plan was a great way to break my habit of checking email and worrying about missing out on the next fabulous new internet meme. Besides – I was on vacation ... come on!

But in truth, it was not a clean getaway. Digital ideas were everywhere, absolutely surrounding me. It was no surprise, for example, that Cape Town has ubiquitous Wi-Fi, and that the preferred method to get around town was to summon an Uber. Even when we were off on safari, digital thinking was prevalent. We met Karen, the Camp Manager with a stellar resume in hospitality (Emirates, Four Seasons, Disney Orlando) and a promising career in management, all while cultivating her ambition to create a software package for hospitality.

Even our safari guides were connected thinkers – spiritual men of the earth, dedicated to the environment and nature. Oats, our first guide, spoke at length about how he will market and sell his elephant repellant idea using YouTube and social media. And TJ, our second guide, noted with irony that he could not buy his favorite bird book locally, even though the author lived a few miles away. He had to order it from Amazon.

Thankfully, Humanity Is Everywhere

At the same time, I was surrounded by reminders of the human element, and the importance of connecting with people. Cape Town and Johannesburg, for example, are amazing cities still actively celebrating their liberation and the memory of Nelson Mandela. In Cape Town, there is a clear focus and visible emphasis on enabling women for success in business and society. And more basic human needs came to the fore; there is still a severe drought in Cape Town, and I grew comfortable taking a shower with a bucket between my legs to catch the extra water, to be used in the gardens of our bed and breakfast. Have you ever spent time in an area dealing with drought? You become hyper-sensitive to your impact on the environment and your place in the community – even if it's a short-term visit!

Humanity is incorporating digital into our thinking, our doing, and our living. It feels natural, and very practical, to incorporate digital thinking into our businesses as well. Digital business is human business. As in life, the two ideas are inextricably linked.

Being Digital in a Human World

Recent technology developments such as AI and Robotics seem to threaten humanity's role in the value chain. While automating work and eliminating people makes for great headlines, the wiser bet on these technologies is that they will augment human effort. These technologies can make us smarter and more able, but they will not replace us.

How do we counter the fear of jobs being replaced by smart machines, robots, and automation? By pointing out that the most impactful applications of this technology are not in replacing humans, but in augmenting their work – doing the rote, repetitive, and labor-intensive stuff, and freeing up our time for analysis, decision-making, value judgment, and deeper insights.

This is the true measure of a "Digital Business" – an organization that embraces digital thinking, process, and technology to create value and deliver on their mission.

A Digital Business will only succeed when it understands how to connect with people. Your Digital Transformation – the process of becoming a Digital Business – will only succeed when it incorporates ideas like human-centered design, tech- and soft-skills development, and a real focus on engagement and inclusion with the people in your company who will interact with these digital tools to get the job done.

Digital business can create real value for all stakeholders – employees, customers, suppliers, shareholders – as long as the human factor of these relationships is kept in mind.

Don't Think So Much!

Before you become overwhelmed with what can seem a daunting task, I say this: *don't think so much*. The problem with most discussions around Digital Transformation is too much theory and not enough practical thinking. This can confuse and complicate some of the core ideas that are already established in your organization's daily work. Too much theory can introduce uncertainty, slowing the change you are trying to enable.

There is a simpler way of understanding the impact of Digital – think of it as more evolutionary than revolutionary for your organization. A simpler, clearer path that is aligned with the goals and strategy of your business, and the people within it, will go a long way toward making your Digital aspirations a reality.

So don't think so much about the process of change. Familiar patterns will emerge, and there are simple, actionable frameworks that will help orient your thinking and help you to align with these patterns. As you keep the focus on the human impact of this change – on your team, your customers, and your stakeholders – you will build a new digital reality that works.

In this book, we are going to dive deep into understanding how to execute a human-centric Digital Transformation for your business. In many ways, you could argue that the process is already underway. We have witnessed an evolution over the past 30+ years in organizations where basic automation, accounting and manufacturing systems, email and e-commerce, and computer-assisted engineering have already made transformative impacts on your operations, your customers, your products, and your employees. But that work may be happening in silos, disconnected from each other, and often is not truly connected to the *people* making this change happen.

This book aims to pull together the threads that have developed over time, connect with the newest enabling technology that is coming into play right now, and tie it all together into an uncomplicated picture. And above all, we will make sure your transformative work has the correct focus on human factors – design, sustainability, and a fully engaged workforce.

Strategy Before Transformation

Chapter 2 will take a few steps back to get the big picture. We will invest a little time getting clarity about the differences between *strategy* and *execution* – terms that are, at times, used interchangeably to ill effect. This book does not attempt to help you develop a Digital Strategy – that is a different conversation, on a completely different level.

There are several paths businesses will take as they approach a Digital Transformation. Some are evolutionary, natural progressions along their current path, while other strategies are disruptive and revolutionary, as external forces present fundamental challenges to your products, your markets, and your customers. It is good to understand how you got to this point (the Why), but this book is primarily focused on the How.

We will also talk about *company culture* – a significant force that can work for and against change and acceptance. This very human aspect of your organization will have a great impact on, and be impacted by, your Digital Transformation.

Five Components

Chapters 3 through 8 get into the structure of your Digital Transformation by describing, in simple terms and meaningful examples, the Five Components of a Great Digital Business. These are the broad chunks of technology, process, skills, and competencies that must come together in a purposeful and mindful manner to enable success for your organization. You will see the expected targets: systems and processes designed to automate, streamline, and produce actionable metrics. But there are important organizational issues to discuss as well. Where does process ownership for digital skills and capabilities typically reside? What strengths and talents do each of the Five Components bring to your Digital Transformation? And where can the different functional areas of the business drive your digital success by bringing their unique strengths and capabilities to the table?

What Can You Do?

Chapters 9 through 11 focus on taking action. What can your teams in all functional areas of the business bring to the table to make this Digital Transformation happen? And how can you get to that "next level" and provide real leadership for the company?

There is no clear and obvious order of events as you start down this path, but there are ample opportunities inside of your organization to share and grow together. Leadership will come from (and be given to) those with the right vision, the right competencies, and the right attitude.

Throughout it all, we will focus on the human part of the conversation, sharing real-world stories and examples that will make these newfangled Digital ideas more relatable and less of a threat.

Who should read this book? Anyone who wants to cut through the hype and the buzzwords, and see things in a simple and actionable way.

- ✓ Entry-level folks who want to *change how things work* (and advance their careers)
- ✓ Mid-level folks who want to *make a difference* (in a relevant and meaningful way)
- ✓ Senior-level folks who want to *lead, innovate, and transform* (before they are forced to follow)
- ✓ Everyone who wants to advance to the next level

Let's get started!

Digital Strategy Versus Digital Transformation

Before we dive into the details of your Digital Transformation, we should spend some time discussing *strategy*. After all, this is a book about *tactics*, and focuses primarily on how to get things done. Before you can define the *How*, you must be clear on the *Why*.

For any business, a clearly defined strategy will give context and guidance for the tactical decisions that are made. In the same way, you must have a solid understanding of what your Digital Strategy is before you can embark on a Digital Transformation.

As noted before, this book does not attempt to help you develop a Digital Strategy. Organizations develop their digital initiatives in many ways; some are natural progressions along their current path, and digital evolution occurs slowly and deliberately over time. Other companies have their Digital Transformation thrust upon them, as disruptive external forces make revolutionary changes and introduce new and different challenges to your products, your markets, and your customers.

It is worth spending some time reviewing how you got to this point, if only to clarify the context and set the stage for the transformation that you are considering. And don't be surprised if you are closer than you think! There may be digital elements in your existing strategic plan already. Then again, if Digital Business is not seen as relevant to how your organization creates sustaining value, it will be difficult to earn focused attention for your ideas.

How We Win

What is the objective of your business strategy? What is the scope and domain of your business? And how exactly will you win? What is the advantage that you will lever to achieve your objectives? This simple approach to defining a strategy[1] provides connection points for introducing Digital thinking to the key stakeholders in your organization:

- **Objective**: How can Digital specifically get you to your objective faster, with better quality and clear value generation?

- **Scope**: What do your customers want? And where else might they get it? Who is your current competition?

- **How We Win**: How might Digital become a new and differentiating feature that creates higher barriers to entry for competitors in established niches, and breaks down those barriers in growth markets?

An alternative impact on your cleanly defined strategy could be a bit more "transformational" – whereby "transformational" I mean, "Let's rip this to shreds before we get disrupted."

Clearly it is not a good idea to rush to your boss with hair afire, excitedly promoting Digital Transformation in an organization that is calmly comfortable with their analog continuity. But our simple strategy breakdown can be used to gently introduce the topic:

---

[1] (Collis and Rukstad 2008)

- **Objective**: How can Digital be used to improve the fundamental value that you can deliver to your customers?

- **Scope**: For your current markets, what disruptions might come from new entrants, unhindered from legacy constraints? Alternatively, what new markets have you not addressed?

- **How We Win**: What happens if you add a new and deeper information component to the depths of your domain experience? Can this become a game-changing competitive advantage?

Yes, there is a conservative "slow road" approach. A tactical focus on optimizing operations with new digital capabilities will create value for the shareholders and stakeholders, and deliver decent earnings growth. It's also a great way to introduce an organization to new and different technology that may be far out of the comfort zone. Do not underestimate fear of the unknown!

But driving profitable growth with all the right adjectives (organic, sustainable, scalable, defensible, etc.) is a powerful motivation. Successful enterprises are typically not driven to "merely exist." The great ones create value for owners, customers, and employees on a consistent and sustainable basis. Most corporate strategies – at least the exciting ones – are focused on this value creation. Adding digital elements can be an important part of changing the fundamental ability of the organization to compete, grow, and prosper in a meaningful way.

Creating Value

As your organization ponders a transformational change toward becoming a Digital Business, a critical strategic concern for the leadership team will be the creation of value. Simply put, *what's in it for the company*? This can be a more nuanced question than one might expect. Are we talking about the value created for the shareholder as we focus on a great stock? Or is it the value created for our employees and our customers as we focus on a great company?

Let's break this into three separate conversations, focused on the three different stakeholders.

Value for Shareholders

Also known as *Shareholder Return*, this is the raw, capitalist form of value creation. How are you building a more valuable company, and driving market value, by adding digital capabilities? There is a ton of information available on what creates long-term shareholder value, but in its simplest form, the value of a stock is driven by three levers:

Earnings Growth: The day-to-day operations of a company, creating and selling products at a fair profit. The objective here is to increase cash earnings, and there are many areas where Digital Business has a direct impact. Historically, automation of internal operations has focused on driving down costs; automation also enables a company to scale their operations, efficiently handling an increase in volume without a corresponding growth in the cost required to support those sales. Customer-facing digital efforts will also impact earnings by driving the quality and volume of sales, gaining share in existing markets, and creating new opportunities with new and innovative offerings.

Capital Efficiency: What does your business do with the cash contributed by shareholders and generated by operations? This lever is primarily controlled by the Finance organization, and when these folks are buying back stock or restructuring corporate debt, it does not feel like there is a big digital play. However, when capital is tied up in inventory, invested in manufacturing capacity, or used to make acquisitions of businesses or intellectual property, properly leveraged digital capabilities will drive return on capital by optimizing inventory and capacity, and streamlining integrations. There will always be a need for efficient operations, plus tight collaboration to pull in new people and new capabilities to your team.

Multiple Expansion is a fancy term for that interesting gap between the imputed value of a company (based on actual performance) versus the current price on the open market. Why are some stocks more highly rated than their peers? What have they done to earn such a high (or low) earnings multiple? Market price can be heavily impacted by the perception of risk and volatility, and the relative performance of your organization versus peers in the market. Your Digital Business can and should focus on managing and reducing risk, as every good business would. Multiple expansion and market sentiment are quite difficult to predict, so it is better to focus on what you can control in your internal operations, the quality of your customer relationships, and the strength of your products in the market. The rest should take care of itself.

We could drill into more of the detail here, but this basic framework can help us answer the first important question: *How are you building a more valuable company, and driving market value, by adding digital capabilities?*

Value for Employees

The counterpoint to a great *stock* is a great *company* – one in which employees have the right skills, the right motivations, and are highly engaged. Employee Engagement is a bit of a buzzword, and when first introduced to an organization, can be a difficult concept to grasp. A basic understanding of Employee Engagement can be achieved by answering three simple questions from the employee's point of view:

Do I understand and believe in the purpose of the company? Do I know where we are going? Clarity of purpose, and a strong sense of direction, brings value to the employee in the form of a clear individual vision, an affirmation of organizational values and, hopefully, alignment with the employee's personal and professional values.

Do I get the support I need from my manager? The individual must shoulder the weight of their roles and responsibilities – this is a job, after all, and not a hobby. Nevertheless, the role of the supervisor or manager is critical, and people expect clear direction, open and honest communication, and solid feedback on their performance.

Do I have the tools and processes needed to be successful at my job? It can be frustrating – and quite disheartening – to be expected to deliver when the tools are inadequate and the processes in place seem to just get in the way. A highly engaging environment makes the right investments in tools, and consistently iterates on and improves on internal and external processes.

With this simple definition, we ask a set of important questions. How are you defining, refining, and supporting the purpose of the company by adding Digital capabilities? Will these changes help or hurt the relationship between teams and their supervisors? And will a Digital Transformation help your employees get the training and support they need to do their very best?

Value for Customer

Engaged employees are critical, but the purpose of a business is to create and sell products and services to their customers. There are two areas in an effective Digital Business that are focused on creating value for the customer.

Connections with Customers: Really listening and understanding their needs, developing products and services that fulfill those needs, with a fanatical focus on customer service.

Information added to Products: The introduction of information as a new and differentiating feature in your products and services can truly change your role in the market, and your value to the customer. In this component of your Digital Business, it is critical to focus on the entire value chain. How can your Product Development and Channel Management teams derive value from this information? What about your channels, including OEMs, distributors, dealers, brokers, your Customers, and your Customers' customers?

The questions that arise here are important – but not as important as where you get your answers. Digital capabilities make it easier than ever to *really listen* to your customers and focus on their needs, but you must turn your attention externally, and focus on where your Customers are!

A Balanced Response

The thoughtful and observant reader should understand that decisions and directions aimed at improving your great company will run counter to the needs of a great stock, and vice versa. A short-term focus on quarterly earnings and cash flows may drive the stock value, but can lead to actions that make it tough on employees and customers alike.

Can an organization survive long term if you keep slashing costs to maintain earnings growth? The math really does not work; you can only cut so far. You need engaged teams, creating dynamite products and terrific customer relationships, to deliver sustainable results.

On the other hand, you are running a business here! There are times when the employee needs the company, and times when the company needs the employee. Some decisions may seem harsh, as when the organization must pivot away from favored customers, fun projects, or exciting markets. And some of these pivots may create change for your teams – change that individuals on your teams will not agree with.

This is the time when strong leadership contributes greatly to the conversation – with open communication and clarity of purpose, and a focus on maintaining that balance.

Great company, great stock... there are plenty of businesses that make this work, but it does take work!

"Born Digital" Versus Traditional Business

Do these strategic digital ideas apply equally to all organizations? Is there really a transformational opportunity for every business, if they just embrace their place in a digital world?

Clearly there are some organizations for whom a Digital Transformation should be a straightforward exercise. For businesses that trade in easily digitized products – publishing, consulting services, or software, for example – what is standing in their way? They have a few puzzle pieces already in place: the product is information-based, and their customer-facing processes are already automated. Some components of digital thinking are already important components of their business model (how they do what they do). It should be a much easier transition to digital thinking for these companies than, say, an old-fashioned industrial manufacturer that ships out pumps or valves or big machines, stamped or cast out of metal, and driven by motors that convert energy into physical action.

It seems logical that a "Born Digital" business might be better suited to a full Digital Transformation, while a traditional manufacturing business would struggle. However, things are not always what they seem. There are multiple components to a Digital Business, and we should not see any one of them as more critical to success than another. A manufacturing firm may have a completely manual process for connecting with their customers (*faxed or phoned-in orders? No problem...*). On the other hand, that same manufacturer may deliver high levels of customer satisfaction with on-time and accurate deliveries, while at the same time keeping inventories low and cash flow high. Such a firm is reliant on well-run systems to automate and optimize their planning, which is a highly digital place to be.

What about technology partners that traffic in digital products and services? Well, how many times have you had to struggle with that boutique consulting firm with a chronic inability to mail invoices on time, where lots of manual processing is required to get the bill right? Just another example of "the cobbler's children have no shoes"!

Few organizations can truly claim to be "Born Digital" but there are simple ways to tell if your firm may have a leg up on the process. Just look at how your teams already think about the value of facts, and the value of people.

Data

How do you think about identifying opportunities to grow revenue? And how do you think about identifying and truly understanding operational problems and how to best address them? You may not have a terrific accounting system for internal processes, or sophisticated customer-facing systems, or digitally enabled products. Even so, do your teams come to the table prepared to answer these questions with hard numbers (where possible) and specific examples (at a minimum)?

If your teams work to target and realize opportunities and solve problems by "speaking in facts" (not opinions), you are in a great spot. Your business is nicely predisposed to understanding the value of data. You just need systems and processes to crunch the data you have, and to collect the data you are missing.

Teams

Regardless of the product, processes, and customers, does your organization value the people on your team? Do you seek to build a diverse team that communicates openly in an environment of trust, where good ideas matter? Do you clearly communicate the mission of the team? Do your managers work to understand how to get the best out of your people? Do you treat people with respect — not coddling them or taking care of their every whim, but by acting with a clear intent and focus on why the business exists in the first place? When your organization pays attention to the people who work there, you are in an excellent position for a Digital Transformation.

Some might argue that the focus on your team, and how they work together in support of the mission of the company, your customers, and the value you deliver with your products, is the most important component of a Digital Business. It certainly is the most important component of a successful Digital Transformation; any level of change impacts people, and requires those people to make the change happen.

In fact, if you are looking for a simple place to start, before you launch into a holistic Digital Transformation, focus on how your teams understand the Why and the How of what you do every day.

It sounds simple, but it will be immediately impactful, and a great first step on your journey[2].

Organizational Structure

Is there an organizational component to the question of applying digital thinking to your strategy? Many companies are considering a decentralized IT model, where IT resources and decisions are pushed down to business units inside the corporation. The same structural approach can be applied to sales and marketing, customer service, or engineering, and essentially puts more decision-making power closer to your customer. Can decentralized digital capabilities work for your business?

This simplistic description masks a lot of detail because terms like *resources, decisions,* and *business units* mean different things to different people. But there are common threads in the discussions that will lead up to this decision, and the options are not entirely black and white.

The decision to centralize or decentralize Digital does not have to be a strictly binary choice between two bad scenarios – an authoritarian, top-down culture of control (that stymies innovation) versus the "wild west" of no standards, no integrations, and no cost leverage (that impedes collaboration). There are pros and cons on both extremes, and like most decisions in business, the optimal truth is somewhere in the middle: a blend of the best ideas, coupled with a thoughtful effort to mitigate the inherent challenges to deliver positive results.

Resource Optimization: Typically, this conversation starts in organizations with centralized functions that struggle to keep up with quickly changing demands. A centralized IT team, for example, may become frustrated because they perceive cost has become the primary driver of investment priorities. It is fascinating to note how quickly IT conversations move to cost control and bottom-line topics. This is why a centralized model is preferred by

---

[2] A powerful technique for leaders to inspire action; from the book Start with Why, by Simon Sinek. (Sinek 2011)

IT – so that we can take advantage of our size to aggregate purchasing power for better pricing.

There are strategic implications as well. Defining clear-cut standards for Digital technology purchases and processes reduces complexity, enables predictability and reliability for core systems, facilitates integration of data and processes, and establishes an environment where collaboration and knowledge sharing can take place. Wouldn't it be better to optimize resources for these core services, freeing up time and investment to drive the top line?

Point of Impact: So why do some folks call out for decentralization? The strategic view is a recognition of the power and value of your customers. A successful organization puts the customer at or near the center of their focus. In this world, the optimal organization moves decision-making power as close to the customer as possible. To remain customer focused, you need to be agile and responsive, and continuously develop processes that deliver value right at the point of impact.

The more tactical view is a practical view. The organization needs or wants new things and better capabilities, but is frustrated by the costs (in time, attention, and money). Why can't everything be as simple as downloading an app?

Searching for Best Practices: When contemplating oversight control of your digital functions, the first step is to realize that there are many viewpoints. Do not assume that any one team has all the answers. Keep an open mind, and look for the tradeoffs.

If the topic of decentralized digital is broached, traditionally centralized teams need to fight the urge to assert control. Do not view decentralization as a challenge to your abilities. It is a recognition that the status quo is limiting the business in some way. Instead, look at this as the start of a healthy conversation about the critical requirements of the business, the assumptions and risks of any decision, and a bit of discovery on best practices.

At the same time, people in the functional areas, product lines, and business units who wish to assert control and make their own decisions need to look at the benefits of the centralized digital option with eyes wide open. Your perception of cost may need to change, since you may lose the leverage of the larger user base in purchasing decisions. And the increased amount of time and energy required to understand the options, implement the systems, and provide ongoing support may be a big surprise.

Impact, Not Control

How to break the impasse? Look to examples from the outside, where applied digital solutions can tell us a lot.

- "Mobile first" strategies point to *decentralization* – specific, limited, focused solutions at the point of impact
- Cloud and "information as a service" concepts point to *centralization* – hugely leveraged support of infrastructure, with tons of flexibility and agility for deployment and support
- Open source technology and Agile development process will lean toward *decentralization*, by empowering the end points to build bespoke solutions to address specific challenges.

None of these examples are clear-cut, and a contrarian case can be made for each.

- "Mobile first" strategies point to *centralization* – delivering predictable results by defining a platform that all digital efforts can leverage for scalable, sustainable, integrated results.
- Cloud and "information as a service" concepts point to *decentralization* – providing smarter components but pushing responsibility for understanding how to apply digital ideas out to the edge, closer to the customer.
- Open source tech and Agile process only work when *centralization* concepts like standard work and strictly documented process enable distributed development.

At the end of the day, the right choice is made by focusing on impact.

> *Aligned with our core objectives (Why) ...*

> *... we can design the best environment and methods (How)*

> *... so we can deliver on our commitments to the Customer (What).*

The alternative is to worry about control ...

> When I can direct the tasks and resources (What),
>
> ... I am better able to pick the methods (How)
>
> ... to deliver on my objectives (Why).

The latter is upside-down, and the thought process is backwards. In so many disciplines, the mantra is always to focus on the objective – the problem we are trying to solve, and the value we are trying to create.

If we base our digital decisions on driving for the biggest impact, we will get better decisions on organization, process, and technology.

Field Notes: How to Teach Innovation

Spoiler alert: It can't be taught ...

An important part of your digital culture – and a critical success factor for humanizing your Digital Business – is encouraging your teams to think more analytically and less literally. Folks need to stop focusing on the mechanical task of *manipulating* data in spreadsheets just to produce the answers they need to see. Instead, you should deliver a deeper level of training, and *learn* to use native query and download tools to pull data from the source system at will. How about *experimenting* with the data, potentially stumbling upon trends and identifying real opportunities?

This is not, by the way, what most people are seeking. They want the organization to learn how to *innovate*, not how to *code*. People take shelter behind literal interpretations, and follow the letter (rather than the spirit) of the law.

Often, coworkers are not always encouraged to *ask questions*, but to *provide answers*. Differentiating between the two is a bit of a gray area, and when time is short and to-do lists are long, the focus will always be on getting *a result*. Not necessarily *the result* or *the best result*, but just *a result*. If you ask for a metric, I will give you the metric; I will not ask the next question.

Here is an example. In one project, I asked folks to eliminate steps in a workflow process. Their solution was to reduce the number of steps in the workflow by *combining multiple tasks* into a single step.

> *Hey, I successfully answered your question. I went from 10 steps to 8.*

Unfortunately, this solution did not reduce the actual work being done, and actually eliminated our ability to analyze time sinks in the process by removing the granularity of the defined steps.

> *But I eliminated a step, just like you asked...*

How do you change people or encourage them to be more innovative? How do you teach intellectual curiosity? In my opinion, traits like innovation, imagination, a sense of adventure, or the willingness to try and fail, really cannot be *taught*. But they can be teased out of people.

There are many classic approaches – establish an environment of innovation, give employees permission to fail, establish audacious goals, etc. But the most important is to lead by example.

Try some little things: rearrange your office, change seats in your team meetings, buy your team lunch. And try some big things: learn how to automate your desktop software using recorded macros, write some collaboration content for the team intranet site, take a customer out to lunch for some blue-sky imagination time on new product features.

But most of all, as you prod, push, pull, and otherwise exhort your team to new ways of thinking, keep an eagle eye out for any little bit of progress in their thinking – a glimmer of off-the-wall innovation – and call it out. We were all kids once, but corporate life kind of beats it out of us. We need to celebrate the little things while people get their sea legs and let their natural impulses take over.

Innovation cannot be taught – you just have to remind folks how fun it can be, and how good *they* can be at it. A great Digital Business will bring this important capability into your culture and make it part of every day.

Chapter 3

The Five Components of a Great Digital Business

Once you have a sense of where Digital will support and/or drive your corporate strategy, it is time to get specific about the tactical details. Once again, this is a relatively new phenomenon. We have all heard many breathless opinions about the "digitization of business" and Digital Transformation; the wondrous innovation possible when a company fully embraces new technology, and incorporates it into the fabric of their go-to-market and operational strategy.

In the end, you are left with fancy slide decks and pithy bullet points that do not say much of anything. Too often they are skewed along a single critical dimension (*information that connects you with your customers... data that transforms your products and markets... analytics that let you see the future...*); ideas and words, but no concrete plans. Usually, "digital strategy" comes across as a sales demo for some cloud or SaaS offering, an introduction to a large and expensive consulting engagement, or maybe a pitch for organizational change as the Marketing group tries to take over IT (or, the IT team makes a play to bring in Marketing).

When you are developing a Digital Transformation for your organization, stay away from technology specifics and org chart jockeying, at least in the beginning. During the strategy conversation, your team should develop a clear vision of what you do, where you play, and how you win. The Digital part of your strategy should focus on higher level issues – the value you deliver and the high-level methods used, target markets and customer types, and winning plays that leverage customer relationships and/or critical product features. When complete, you will have a better idea of the critical areas of your business that can and should leverage connection, collaboration, and intelligence.

From Strategy to Tactics

Now that we have your Digital Strategy defined, we are ready to discuss tactics. How will you transform into a Digital Business to deliver the strategy? The implementation plan for an effective and impactful Digital Business[3] will incorporate these functional areas:

Internal Operations

Do your teams really understand the systems and processes that automate internal transactions – the details of running your business every day – and use them to their full potential? This covers an amazing range of systems, from the daily and mundane (email, calendaring, basic communications) to accounting systems that tick and tie your order-to-cash, purchase-to-pay, and make-to-ship processes (aka Enterprise Resource Planning, or ERP). Most established companies have reasonably mature systems and processes in place. The "revolution" here will focus on deeper training, richer data, and integrations with other systems.

---

[3] (MacLennan, The Five Core Components of a Great Digital Business 2016)

Customer Relationships

From call centers and outbound marketing efforts, to websites and e-commerce tools that bring product information directly to your end customers and distribution channels (and return detailed feedback in the process), to CRM systems that help you track and analyze complex market relationships – data-enabled connections can tie you tightly with your customers and help you grow. But have you connected with systems for internal operations to eliminate transactions and "touches," and bring velocity to your value creation? And can you move beyond transactions to develop tighter relationships with customers – maybe bringing them into product development or strategic planning?

Products and Services

Why limit yourself to operations and customers? Information about your products and how they are operating in the field is becoming easier to gather, and is quickly becoming an assumption in the marketplace. Can you generate new forms of revenue, deliver differentiating features in your products and services, and redefine your customers' expectations to build a protective moat around your business?

In many companies, these three core areas of the business have been loosely connected at best. But when you tightly integrate your Digital Business with free-flowing, consistent, detailed information between people working in Manufacturing, Customer Service, Marketing, Engineering, and New Product Development, all three of these core areas (operations, customers, and products) will see significant improvements in productivity, customer satisfaction, and revenue growth.

This is a significant step forward, but functional transformation and integration is not enough. Relying on integrated, consistent data flowing through all systems is one thing, but leveraging that data for insights and opportunities does not come automatically. A scalable and sustainable Digital Business will also target how people work, and how people work together.

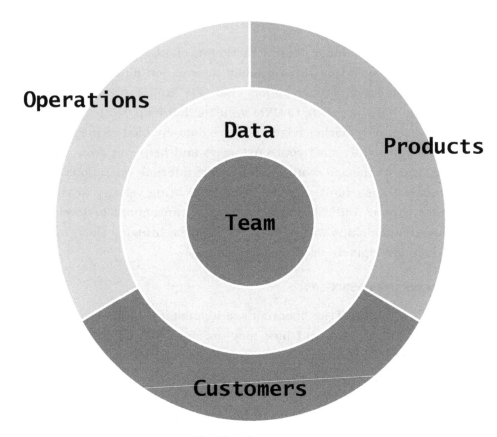

The Five Components

Data and Analytics

Access is only half the battle. To realize the full benefit, decision makers and influencers will need to truly understand how to work with the data, asking it questions and working out the answers. And this will not work if you are going to be like every other organization, relying on a small core of data wizards and report writers for the analytics. High-performing individuals and teams must be able to access and manipulate information quickly and effectively on their own with minimal dependence on external resources. This challenge has less to do with fancy visualization tools, and much more to do with applied domain expertise, specific skills training, and genuine intellectual curiosity. People need to take ownership of their data in every sense of the word.

Building Great Teams

You must always stress this theme: it may seem counterintuitive at first, but a deeply digital world relies on *people* – individuals with advanced skills and learning agility, working in distributed teams across multiple locations, collaborating and sharing in an effective and fluid manner. This is much tougher than it sounds, as there are many societal factors that must be overcome. But when you crack this code, and bring highly engaged teams together, your buzzword targets (*Innovation! Engagement! Productivity! Growth!*) will sound less like wishful thinking, and more like success metrics.

Your Digital Strategy statement has to explain what you are trying to achieve, where you will play, and how you will win. But if you are trying to really transform your company, a great Digital Business will nail each of these five components.

- ✓ *How you work*
- ✓ *Who you serve*
- ✓ *What you deliver*
- ✓ *Using data to your advantage*
- ✓ *The people that make it happen*

The Human Elements that Tie It Together

A Digital Business is built on these five components, and the simplicity may feel a bit too reliant on systems and processes. It is time to discuss the most important element that binds them together – people. Where is the humanity that drives our digital decisions and actions?

Knowledge

First, let's think about systems and processes – the core of the first three components (Operations, Customers, and Products). Obviously, people are important to your current internal operational processes. But how dependent are you on those key employees, the critical few who understand how everything works together? How many of your customer connections are based solely on the relationships of your business development team? How much of your product development roadmap is based on that one engineer who knows, and really lives, in the minutiae of the operational parameters of your product?

Your current systems and processes – running internal operations, connecting with your customers, and differentiating your products and services – are highly dependent upon people to make things work. And people, as we are often reminded, are the most expensive components of your P&L.

But be careful to avoid making the illogical leap that so many organizations do: an effective digital world is *not* free from humans. You should not assume that information and technology can or should replace the people in your organization. These capabilities exist to augment and support them.

Effective digital transformation allows you to focus on automating rote work tasks, capture past history and best practices so you do not repeat the same mistakes, and create scalability by making expertise transferable. Armed with these types of enabling digital capabilities, you will be in a position to truly differentiate and create sustainable value for customers and stakeholders.

All five components of your Digital Business (Operations, Customers, Products, Data, and Teams) have pools of knowledge that are trapped in people's minds, on their desks, and in their email inboxes. And your successful Digital Transformation will liberate this trapped knowledge and multiply its impact. The result: teams can quickly pivot to higher value operational tasks, more important customers, and more profitable products.

Skills

Think about the *skills* required to make these digital dreams a reality. When looking in depth at the Data component, you will see that the focus must be on enabling value by building a team with the right set of skills. A Digital Transformation brings new techniques that must be mastered, just like a new machine tool in the shop, a new communication method to reach customers, or a new method to manage the email flooding your inbox every day.

Some of these skills are new, just like the enabling technology that makes change and disruption possible. Other skills are maturing, with updated requirements based on changes in the appetites of your markets and customers. And there is an amazing shortfall of available, skilled labor in technology areas that are well established, or even considered to be "legacy." Increased demand for digital skills has tightened the supply even further, and filling these gaps becomes a familiar task and a critical expectation for aspiring Digital Businesses.

All five components call for specific, valuable, and varied skills to deliver on your opportunities. A training and development process that values skills and encourages growth will enable your Digital Business to scale as fast as the technology.

Values and Culture

A great Digital Business cannot sustain itself when it relies on one or two key people who have all the magic. Instead, you must focus on teams – those that perform the operations that power your business, that connect and engage directly with your customers, and that build and support the products and services that your company delivers. When connected and engaged teams of people join together with a shared vision, they deliver results.

A significant element of how your team comes together will be a consistent set of values and a clearly defined culture. Values represent who you are and how you intend to behave, with your company, your customers, and your community. And culture acts as the adaptive glue that binds everyone together – setting expectations, including all voices, and embracing the diversity that will carry you through opportunities, challenges, and change.

The teams that deliver individual components of your Digital Business will bring uniquely applied values and varying views on culture. Your Digital Transformation must be mindful of this, and blend the work of these different groups into a harmonious whole.

Chapter 4

Digital Operations

History and Context

The first three components of your Digital Business are the things you might expect: systems and processes that automate internal operations, tightly connect you with customers, and change the fundamental nature of your products. These components are directly tied to the history of information and technology and its impact on business – specifically, how organizations compete and win.

Over the years, Michael Porter has documented three transformational waves brought about by advances in technology. The first[4] was in the 1950s and 1960s when systems were developed to automate critical parts of the internal value chain, from finance and accounting to supply chain planning and

---

[4] (Porter and Millar, How Information Gives You Competitive Advantage 1985)

optimization. These early replacements for ledgers and pegboards have grown into the behemoths of Enterprise Resource Planning (ERP) that we know today: highly complex systems that seek to automate every facet of your internal operations from Order-to-Cash, Purchase-to-Pay, Make-to-Ship, and Record-to-Report.

There are many more areas where digital systems have been developed to automate internal operations. The common denominator of most of this work is the great rush to productivity – the ability to do more with less. But another transformational change came about when businesses turned their sights on internal communication processes. Can you remember the days of printed memos, physical bulletin boards, and the importance of administrative staff to answer the phones? When email was introduced to the organization, the old guard scoffed at the idea of typing their own messages and sharing their Rolodexes. Fast forward 30 years, and the ubiquity and importance of email is both staggering. A critical system for the operation of most companies, email has evolved into the core communication tool, workflow enabler, and knowledge store for organizations everywhere.

Communications and desktop productivity fall into this first component of Digital Transformation. Technology that connects your internal processes – and the people that rely on them – is the second major digital platform that your company relies on, after ERP, accounting, and supply chain systems.

It is important to note that this technology has its roots in the personal computer revolution of the late 1980s. From the beginning, people took the name of this enabling technology to heart. *(This is my personal computer – completely mine to manage, as unique and valuable as my favorite red stapler.)* More significantly, these new machines were a revolutionary break from the corporate number-processing behemoths that were centrally controlled in cold, pristine rooms by mysterious men in white lab coats. On the contrary – these machines had personality (and played Solitaire).

The controls and process that ERP automation imposed were binary, antiseptic, impersonal, and focused on eliminating waste. This was a huge change from the organic, flowing, adaptive business environment of the past when things were a bit looser, a bit friendlier, and a lot more "lossy." The PC brought back some of that individuality, along with a lack of tight controls. In a way, this was an early form of digital innovation – a change in the environment that enabled truly new ways of thinking and working.

This may be an interesting retrospective, but business and culture has moved forward in 30 years, and expectations have changed. It is difficult to imagine running a business without these types of systems, and businesses today are confidently realizing huge value from their old-school digital platforms. Personal technology has changed as well, as hardware and communications advancements have brought the smartphone. These miracle devices have unchained us from the desktop and ushered in unprecedented physical freedom. This has not been without some cost, however; concerns around cybersecurity, intellectual property, privacy, and financial controls have morphed our thinking around what it means to be a connected individual.

Current State – Strengths and Weaknesses

The business world continues to adapt and optimize information technology for internal operations. As you incorporate this first component into your Digital Transformation, you need to understand and take advantage of the inertial forces of change when you can. You should ask: what are the impactful, scalable, and sustainable best practices here?

No one wants to remember the pain of their first (and often, last) ERP implementation, but it is important to understand your current state at that same level of detail. How have your teams taken advantage of this huge investment in time, money, and people? Are you focused solely on the tasks required to flow data cleanly to your general ledger so you can efficiently close the month and update your financial statements within a few business days? It is common for organizations to look on these processes as necessary evils – a sort of transactional overhead that gets in the way of great customer relationships.

But smart teams understand how these systems drive their business while making things much more observable and manageable. It's the difference between people who know their jobs and those who really *understand* their jobs. It is the difference between knowing the tasks that need to be completed, and truly understanding how you can use information, transactions, and processes to drive efficiencies and increase customer service.

Imagine the operations of a large distribution company, with 100 manufacturing locations across multiple time zones, producing a broad range of products for the company's catalog. These are low-margin, high-volume products (*"We sell truckloads, not pallets!"*), and your customer relies heavily on your products to serve *their* customers every day. But delivered cost is important, so shipping full truckloads is desired. And expectations are high for product availability and on-time delivery. Competition will promise the moon, and you need the ability to respond.

Now, you could ensure 100 percent on-time delivery by carrying loads of inventory. But carrying costs will cut into your margins, and inventory values will load down the balance sheet.

How do companies balance customer requirements, operational costs, and financial expectations? With systems that do the heavy computational lifting, optimizing inventory levels against costs and customer demand. It is a data-dependent process that crosses organizational boundaries, and requires crisp communications and fluid data sharing between different parts of the organization.

Supply Chain Management is an excellent example of a digital business process that can be difficult to enable. Common challenges to many internal processes include very human-focused concerns.

Usable: Is the process complex to execute and difficult to teach to new employees? Are standard process guides available, or does training consist of "following that person around" until the new person picks up the steps?

Data-driven: Touchless automation, complex optimizations, and actionable analytics are heavily dependent on complete and correct data. "Garbage in, garbage out" is a real problem; does your team truly understand the sources and uses of the data they are creating and maintaining?

Sustainable: Are internal systems and processes overly dependent on individual expertise? Is there complexity that does not add value? Can you see this process scaling to handle 10x the order volume, 50x the customers, 100x the products? Can we build a team that can handle the change?

Over time, your Operations teams have developed skills that are crucial for the smooth operation of your business. These skills can be leveraged quite effectively by the other components of your Digital Business.

Project Management and Communicating Complexity: There are few projects more complex than the implementation of a new ERP system, a new financial reporting system, or even a new email platform. Technology that touches the lives of many people requires coordination, planning, and change management that is as well designed as the systems you are rolling out, along with plenty of mindful, aware communication.

Financial Controls, Security, Privacy: Financial Reporting, Internal Audit, Compliance, Legal, and Cybersecurity are an interesting set of competencies you may not fully appreciate. But years of regulations, compliance requirements, and changing expectations have honed their skills. Focusing on privacy and security often feels like it is stifling digital innovation. That may be so, but it is part of the landscape. Your Digital Transformation can accelerate by pulling in the right skills and experience from these important teams.

The Link to Digital Business

Do not think of the digital processes that support your Operations as overcomplicated, expensive, and tedious. These systems are foundational, even instructional, for the "sexier" components (... *Mobile!... AI!... IoT!...*) of your Digital Business conversation.

Admittedly, the technology seems mundane and dated – an uninspiring front end to the boring transactional detail of daily commerce, and a cost of doing business in the modern world. But there is a great opportunity here to leverage your organization's knowledge and rigor around data quality, standard work, and transactional discipline.

Customer Relationships

Organizations that are efficient and proficient with their ERP have known for years that the quality of the master data (chart of accounts, bills of materials, details of the item master, etc.) have a significant impact on making the business visible and enabling detailed insights.

There are typically lots of processes specifying the data required to make and ship your products. But what about the data required to market and sell? How can you implement digital catalogs and configuration tools that are truly helpful for customers if you do not have that same level of data-engineering rigor? It is a significant new skill for Sales and Marketing, and the Operations team can help guide the way.

Products and Services

Adding information, analytics, and other data services as a new, highly profitable line item on a monthly invoice sounds simple. But what about all of those "exception" processes like contract pricing, customer returns and exchanges, and even technical support?

When the Engineering, Sales, Customer Service, and Product Support teams truly understand how everything hooks together in the ERP, they will bring huge value to the Product Development team as they define the processing and costs involved in such an offering.

Leveraging Information

As ERP systems have successfully matured beyond the simple view of automating the general ledger, the best teams are using the information to identify costs and opportunities for the bottom line. At the same time, planners are aggressively looking at the entire supply chain and distribution channels, searching for ways to optimize working capital and improve the balance sheet. These are powerful skills that can be transferred to the customer-facing and product line teams working in this new Digital reality.

The Hidden Treasure

As organizations develop skills, knowledge, and understanding (transactional discipline, data quality and governance), they build up a significant asset: rich information in their internal systems.

Leveraging that rich information is a great place to start your digital journey, because to a great extent, your efforts will be hidden from prying, external eyes. Undoubtedly, you can (and will) make some mistakes along the way. You might, for example, disappoint a few customers with missing components, late shipments, or other problems. But that is significantly better than making a mistake in the data driving your e-commerce system, and having that mistake immediately published to the web for everyone to see. And wouldn't you rather work out your sensor, communication, and data management problems with internal equipment *before* impacting hundreds of customers with product problems?

Start with the digital foundation of your internal operations – it is familiar ground. But quickly expand your world view; what you do inside your four walls can inform and drive what you do with customers and products.

Organization and People

As you consider this first component of your Digital Business, think about a few important organizational ideas. First and foremost, who is leading the charge when it comes to systems for internal Operations? Who really "owns" this domain? Typically, ERP systems are introduced by the Finance team, with a desire for monetary and security controls, an ability to streamline reporting processes, and simplifying their planning and analysis tasks. Finance brings a lot to the table for Digital Business; you will need their expertise to build a business case for digital projects and products, expressed in the language and culture of your company.

Your internal IT team is also going to be a big player in this component. Let's face it: the folks who really understand the information flows, the impacts of changes, and the integrated nature of data are the people who are debugging things when they go wrong. When people from different functional teams want to extract data from the system, they are usually working with the IT team to write queries and dump data into spreadsheets for sorting, searching, and computing. And the IT group is typically where the most project management experience resides, with a strong focus on communicating in a complex environment.

Do not forget the Operations teams, especially Planning and Customer Service. It does not take long to realize that these systems can really mess things up if not used correctly. Additionally, when customer demand or supplier variability create real risks for customer satisfaction, Planning and Customer Service folks know how to use the system to solve knotty problems and keep customers happy.

But the best skills of your Operations team are not limited to their facility on the keyboard. Find a company that has experience with the principles and processes of Lean Manufacturing. Daily Management, for example, is an effective piece of the Lean toolkit that pulls people together on the shop floor, directly at the point of impact, and focuses the conversation on what will be required to hit goals and deliver on promises to the customer. When operational processes are mature, the conversations are on point, blunt but not insulting, and focused on solving problems and making improvements. Some of the information comes from the systems, but the most valuable feedback comes from the face-to-face conversations and problem solving that happen on the shop floor.

Operations provide the core data and systems for your Digital Transformation. When done well, it can serve as a foundational example of people, open communication, and personal connections having a huge impact in driving real value.

Field Notes: How To Be Taken Seriously

Part of the challenge for non-customer facing groups like IT, Finance, and Operations is bringing new digital ideas to other areas of the organization. Even though their ideas are backed with a solid understanding of your company and your culture, it is still quite common to see Sales, Marketing, and Product Development teams hiring external consulting groups for the more interesting and exciting projects.

Internal teams are often challenged by a lack of "latest and greatest" digital skills, available cycles to take on the extra work, or communication and marketing experience. But there is another set of skills – a subtler, more enlightened way of engaging with leadership – that is differentiating. And not all external firms have these skills; businesses often have preferred external partners that demonstrate partnership and empathy better than their competition (*"They are good ... and they 'get me' ..."*).

I know a General Manager who has a simple way of testing for a preferred Digital partner by looking for these attributes:

- **Sense of Urgency**: It is not acceptable to start talking about a project in April, only to find out that my team cannot start until September. (*"If you want to stay relevant, there must be some empathy with my 'need for speed,'"*)
- **Business Acumen**: The conversation should really focus on functional priorities and requirements, and not get caught up in new technology. "Shiny objects" can often be a distraction.
- **Creativity**: The team should have a sense of art and design, and be able to flip between out-of-the-box and drive-for-results at the right times. (*"We are typically looking for something differentiating. But at the same time, let's keep things practical and sustainable...."*)
- **Cost for Value**: Effective partners will address this moose on the table by quantifying the return on investment (a framework, algorithm, or model for specifying where value is created, or what the impact will be).

So how can internal Operations teams break through this most-favored-nation roadblock and get involved in more of these projects? The simplest approach is to run to the most difficult part of the list for the external firms: *Cost for Value.*

The internal IT team will say things like "not until September" because they assume the zero-cost option, where all work will be completed by internal people. These folks are already on the payroll, so there is *no incremental cost to get them involved.* And if Marketing has plenty of budget for external resources? Well, why not invest for the long term by trying a staff augmentation arrangement? Have the internal team do the digital work, while using the project budget to pay for backfill resources to cover the internal teams' regular duties. This would be a terrific win, delivering all the value for a lower cost, while freeing up internal resources who truly understand the domain and culture, and know how to get things done quickly in their native environment.

I am amazed that most software, hardware or services technology firms rarely provide well-structured cost justification models for their products. Concepts like Value Selling have been well established. Why is it so rare to see simple, glib financial models for these very expensive projects?

Internal Operations teams should be able to win at this game by providing a fully loaded Cost-to-Build and Cost-to-Maintain budget that clearly lays out the cost/benefit for an option. It is better to have this fuller picture upfront than to be sucked into a long-term commitment with a lowball opening price.

This "transparency" is the most underutilized "competitive advantage" that an internal Operations teams can leverage. When the company understands the total cost to implement and to operate a given idea by understanding the real hourly rate being paid for internal labor, a surprisingly effective dollars-and-sense business case emerges to bring Operations teams into the Digital Transformation effort.

Field Notes: The Value of Great Training Material

Truly effective training material is difficult to create and difficult to share, but solid, effective training material is easy to recognize. It typically falls into the "I will know it when I see it" category, and the inherent value seems obvious to most.

If this is true, why are so many businesses trimming their training budgets and underemphasizing these all-important deliverables within their projects? Training material becomes the critical connection between *creating* digital processes and *implementing* them successfully. So why is this undervalued?

Part of the problem may be the difficulty in identifying a tangible benefit. Most projects are subject to some cost-justification pressures, and when hard-dollar benefits are tough to identify, the project costs must be cut. Unfortunately, this typically results in reduced resources for full system tests, training materials, and knowledge transfer.

But is it really that difficult to identify the real value being created by effective training? We walked through this thought exercise during the planning stages of a project.

- The best way to train someone is to dedicate a knowledgeable person to demonstrate the various operations step by step, one by one.
- To replicate that level of attention, a typical project requirement would be two hours of dedicated trainer time per end user.
- Factor in travel time and other things, and you can probably train three people per day per trainer.

So, for an end-user base of 100 people and two trainers, figure on chewing up a solid month of calendar time and devoting two trainers to a grueling schedule. And, for many companies, there will be travel involved, stretching the project timeline even more.

An excellent way to slash the time required would be dedicating one person to the task of creating quality training materials, including step-by-step instructions, samples, screen prints, and video walk-throughs. One person can accomplish a lot in 40 hours of dedicated effort! When finished, all 100 people could take this two-hour, self-directed training class over the course of a week, fitting it in with their regular tasks.

Using this approach, my team and I could see the benefits immediately. The most significant value came in three areas:

- ✓ We eliminated most of the travel expense;
- ✓ We eliminated the need to take two employees off the line for two months to train others; and
- ✓ We slashed the time required to deliver training in half.

You can tweak the math in many ways. For example, calculate the cost of conducting training in a classroom setting, spending 10 days (not 100) of the trainers' time, teaching class sizes of 10 students each. This may improve students' attitudes, since they are getting away from the daily grind – and this may result in better retention of the knowledge.

However, that is not a fair comparison, because the time, attention, and immediate feedback that each student receives will still be more expensive (in time and money) when compared to a well-structured, well-written training piece. In addition, the well-written document can be called upon whenever needed in the following months, after the original trainers have returned to their regular jobs, and the expected, normal level of staff turnover occurs.

Note that we did not calculate all sorts of miscellaneous costs like travel, paper, or lunches for the classroom, nor did we count the value of having ready access to the training material for follow-up training. These costs and benefits are real, but usually not material. We have learned not to sweat the small stuff.

We also learned that results speak volumes. These savings are real, and the effort created value that kept generating returns over many months. In retrospect, the most challenging part was the creation of the training material. Most people are far more comfortable sharing their knowledge in conversations rather than through a written document, so it can be difficult to find someone with this unique skill.

In short, chalk up training and the development of training materials as another important skill required for Digital Transformation.

Chapter 5

Connecting with Customers

History and Context

Digital thinking entered the business world more than 40 years ago when our attention turned to the automation of internal operations. This is the most mature technology in your organization – and also, quite possibly, the most *boring* component of your Digital Business.

Let us turn our attention to the customer-facing, customer-centric processes in your company, with their own collection of supporting systems and derived data. These are quite possibly the most *over-simplified* digital components, going well beyond websites and mobile apps. This next component of your Digital Business introduces some decidedly non-technical *human* elements into your thinking.

Customer-facing technology has been around for many years, and represents the second impact wave of information and technology on the world of business. In 2001, Michael Porter wrote another important article[5] in the Harvard Business Review about how the Internet would enable a new level of connectivity between companies and their value chains[6] (going back to their suppliers, and forward to their customers). Mass customization and the power of the consumer were big ideas, but they strained against the legacy of standardization and control from those monolithic ERPs.

The Internet became a two-pronged way for Marketing, Communications, and really anyone else in the organization to take more control of their digital world. Inexpensive web servers on nimble hosting providers were just a credit card away, and clearly beyond the control of the IT department. This happy level of ownership allowed complete freedom for technically adept people to quickly come up with interesting and compelling replacements for expensive marketing brochures and glossy corporate reports. It was clear that these kinds of systems were not transacting business with customers or impacting the financials in any way, so the level of oversight demanded by Finance and IT was minimal.

As time went on, the two-way nature of this important new channel became apparent. Savvy marketers found that tracking visitor data was easy and quite valuable, giving them insight into what their customers were truly interested in learning. The ability to reach into a customer's attention stream gave Marketing the ability to have a specific, pointed conversation about exactly what was on the customer's mind while they were searching for your products. A company's digital storefront became the perfect place to hear the Voice of the Customer, and helped the company better understand how to keep their customers close.

Over time, the sophistication of web-based applications and services has far exceeded those initial offerings. One of the most striking examples is the concept of the *order configurator*. Think about those websites that allow you to build the custom motorcycle, shoe, or computer of your dreams, with every fancy

---

[5] (Porter, Strategy and the Internet 2001)

[6] (Porter and Millar, How Information Gives You Competitive Advantage 1985)

feature that you might want, in the color and style that you prefer. These applications are powerful tools that pull customers in and make it easy for them to do business with you. These digital tools create "customer stickiness," a cute reference to the highly valuable concepts of customer loyalty and repeat business.

Most ERP veterans will point out that order configurator (aka CPQ, or *Configure Price Quote*) modules within the ERP are notoriously difficult to set up and maintain, because of the detail required to correctly connect all the options with their related (and required) components. But the value here is not limited to *accuracy* – the idea that these websites will make sure all orders get all these rules right. The more powerful observation is that there are *no user instructions* on these websites! A ton of attention has been paid to information and process flow, and how the customer interacts with the system. And the best of these sites take the most complex customer journeys in your business and make them easy enough for your customers to perform without any assistance.

This is the significant capability brought by the Customer component of your Digital Transformation – the idea of *design*. This is not limited to subjective conversations about picking the right colors or debating the correct use of the company logo and brand. We are really talking about process design, information design, and usability. Often referred to as *design thinking*, it focuses our attention on how real human beings use and interact with an operational process, a product, and a set of data. We must be mindful of how people understand and consume this information in the most impactful and effective way.

Another important digital link for many companies is the smartphone, which today is feeding our fascination with mobility and mobile applications. These important customer connection points are not as mature as their web-based predecessors; the introduction of the iPhone in 2007 brought this revolutionary new pathway to market.

Consider the typical mobile app. The most effective ones focus on a small number of specific actions. If a company or organization has several interaction paths, they will often create multiple mobile apps to get the jobs done.

Compare and contrast this to "traditional" web applications and "legacy" client-server or desktop programs. These systems typically present the user with a menu bar across the top, featuring a wide array of functions, processes, and transactions. There is one screen, and one user interface that covers all needs.

But in the world of mobile applications, design thinking has truly come to the fore. Thoughtful developers pay attention to the physical interface (the small screen) and where, when, and how people will interact with the app. It is better to deeply understand how your end customer is going to use this information or application in real life, and design the application to facilitate that use.

Current State – Strengths and Weaknesses

The Customer component of a Digital Business can transform the way we create value for our customers, our employees, and our shareholders. But similar to the Operations component, there are opportunities for improvement – specifically, opportunities to leverage the capabilities and strengths of the other four components.

Speed vs. Integration

The advent of the web gave us a new way to connect with customers. It also saw technology vendors perfect the tactic of bypassing IT to get to the real decision makers (i.e. those who own the budget). Notwithstanding the IT department's feelings, this was actually a good thing, as real progress was being made in improving customer connections. This *need for speed* also translated into the core project methodologies that marketing folks fell in love with – "agile" techniques that promised a fast-twitch development process with quick turnarounds for ever-changing requirements.

But these newly formed teams, with non-traditional technical backgrounds and a fluid set of demands and requirements, often have trouble reconciling the need for engineering and control with the need for speed, flexibility, and a real focus on the customer. Is it surprising that, over time, these disconnected teams have built disconnected processes and data pools?

To be fair, the original vision for most customer-facing systems did not include the aggregation of customer data with operational and product data into a single pool of information that could be leveraged across all functional areas. They were built to connect with our customers in significantly advanced ways, and our access to this data has exceeded our original understanding. As your business becomes holistically digital, you have to think of these systems a bit differently, including how you build, manage, and integrate with them.

The Power of Design

The bigger platform shift has been to mobile: access to ubiquitous mid- to high-bandwidth data coverage; the social shift to a reliance on smartphones for constant connection and ready information; and a consistent expectation of highly integrated information. Customers are expecting, even demanding, a different kind of communication from their suppliers. Specifically: how we inform and educate them with data that is rich, transparent, and augmented by the wisdom of the crowd[7]; how we transact with them through a process that is seamless, cashless, and secure; and how we support them with knowledge that is prescient, effortless, and timely.

This is a high set of expectations from your customers – expectations that you will need to deliver. Design Thinking becomes a critical enabling skill, and a required way of thinking if you hope to deliver on these expectations. But Design Thinking is

---

[7] Refers to the collective opinion of a group of individuals, rather than that of a single expert.

not all that is required. Data management process and technical skill are also key pieces of the puzzle.

Design is an important part of the user experience, the employee experience, and the "stickiness" factor of any process. Customer-facing systems are typically where design gets the credit it deserves. But do not oversell the importance of design. It is not the only tail that wags this dog.

Design requires Data

Fast forward to present day; e-commerce and CRM projects have successfully established that a business can and should have deeper, collaborative relationships with their Customers. But transaction complexity and demand for flexibility increases as these systems have invaded a broader range of industries.

The industrial world, for example, with highly engineered and broadly variable products and services, brings a different level of required sophistication for users of these systems. Consider the example of an e-commerce platform, presenting the aforementioned family of industrial products available for purchase. Most people are familiar with catalog systems for consumer products, with easy-to-use product filtering and selection methods that efficiently narrow the choices down to the ones that best fit the requirements. This level of filtering and selection requires a broadly based and rigorously maintained set of attributes – a level of rigor that industrial companies do not often possess.

Most organizations have processes in place to manage the data required to *make and ship* their products. But that is entirely different from the data required to *market and sell* their products – data that is rarely kept in the ERP system, nor is it maintained with the same rigor. More often than not, small- to mid-size firms will manage this data in spreadsheet lists or document files used to create print catalogs. These are maintained with processes designed for monthly publication calendars instead of an always on, always available, constantly updated, web-based electronic catalog.

Field Notes: It's Design, not Decorating

My daughter works in interior design. When she was just starting out, she liked to remind me that her industry was, at times, misunderstood. She often made me repeat her favorite quote: "It's design, not decorating."

Interior Design is not about simply picking colors and throwing some pillows around the room – she needed to understand how people would use a space. Her work with medical and health centers was amazing. She talked about how the foot traffic would flow, what the environment would be inside and outside, materials and textures to be used, and a million other things that would have real impacts on how effective people would be in their work, how they would care for the sick, and how they would live better in the spaces that she designs.

Obviously I am proud, impressed, and a little bit intimidated by her skills!

I see parallels to these ideas while driving Digital Transformation in the organizations with whom I work. For example, I will often get into conversations about how things are presented on the screen. On mobile apps or web pages, for internal or external audiences, there is a consistently high level of interest in having a say about how something looks. I have found, however, that when someone does not do this for a living, most of their conversation goes to color choices and the layout of things on the screen. Decisions are made because "it seems to look good there." This quickly becomes a very subjective process, which can be quite frustrating, especially for a first-time launch of a mobile app or webpage.

The primary question for the user interface designer is, *"What action are you trying to guide or support?"* The good designer will focus on how effectively people interact with the application. Can they get the things done that *they* want to get done? Will they get things done that *you* want them to get done?

The entire process must start with a clear understanding of the desired outcomes: What actions do you want to guide, facilitate, or make as easy as possible? There is an end goal in mind, a purpose. Design should be purpose driven, while decorating is subjective. Design is how things work, and how things work effectively. Decorating is how things look. Look and feel is part of the conversation for sure, but it is a smaller part of a larger whole.

The design nuances of look/feel and a well-guided process can be tough to teach. But it is very important to give people a chance to have some input on how things look and how things work; this new process will become their own. When they are part of the design process, they will be invested in it, take some ownership, and help push it to the broader organization.

I like to start with some examples of look and feel; it is important to get something up on the screen, just to get an idea of what is possible and give folks a chance to get involved. Most people are intimidated by a blank sheet of paper, but they have no problem editing an existing document. Take advantage of that tendency, and throw something on the screen that is a rough estimate of what is possible. You can inject as much of your own subjectivity as you like, but use it to start the conversation. *"I think this looks good on the screen, do you? Is this effective or not?"* Do not worry if people start changing things. Your objective has nothing to do with fancy awards for a witty design. The real goal is to guide the user, reader, and customer to successfully get a piece of work done.

Learn by doing, get the team involved, and show by example that the design of the process is much more nuanced, more powerful, and more impactful than just "the right shade of blue."

The Link to Digital Business

Most folks fully understand that customer-facing systems belong in your Digital Business. But what roles will those systems play? And how will they interact with and leverage the data and process of the other components?

Internal Operations

The transaction systems that fuel the core processes of Make-to-Ship are wonderful sources of rich data about your customers. Who is buying? More specifically, who is placing the order? What is your performance record with them – are you on time or chronically late? What is the buying history (and patterns) of these customers? And how profitable are they? Are they worth the expense required to keep serving them? That last question explores the idea that some customers are more profitable or valuable than others, and that is an important thing for your organization to know.

Products and Services

Where exactly are your customers using your product? How often? And are your products and services delivering the value promised? These customer touch points can be tracked, studied, and analyzed for those all-important insights to help understand the value you bring, the problem you solve, and the future innovations you can bring to those same customers.

Leveraging Information

You probably see the pattern here – the components of your Digital Business are extending the ecosystem of information, building a rich and detailed picture of your customers, their needs and demands, and their experience with your product and your team. An important part of any company's mission will be its relationships with customers. Leveraging the information gathered around these customers will generate tremendous value, if done correctly.

The Hidden Treasure

Just as the Operations component has an untapped resource in the interesting data generated every day by our internal systems, a similar dynamic is happening with digitally enabled customer relationships. There is magic, and huge opportunity, in applying the core value of your Customer component to internal systems and processes.

Can we apply design thinking to our internal processes? The answer is an emphatic YES, and it may not be that big of a step for many organizations. Smart companies around the world are applying concepts of Lean Manufacturing to streamline operations, eliminate waste, and drive value. Are you doing the same for your digitally enabled internal processes? Companies can and should leverage their experiences in websites and mobile apps, applying them to internal transactional screens. Taking this one step further, companies should clearly communicate internal processes to employees with the same level of rigor that you communicate to your external customers.

Digital has transformed the way we *listen* to our customers, and Design Thinking has transformed the way we *speak* to our customers. Was this an unintended consequence of the advent of the web? Maybe, but let's really take things to a different place and apply Design Thinking to our internal processes, focusing on our employees' engagement in the same way that we focus on our customers' experience.

Organization and People

For the Customer component of your Digital Business, it is clear where the ownership lies. Your Sales and Marketing teams, as noted above, have introduced customer-facing technology with measurable success. But these valuable initiatives have brought a certain amount of organizational angst to the relationship between Marketing and the other functional areas in the business. Operations would like to see better demand information, IT would appreciate predictability and stability with the tech, and Finance is always asking about the return on investment.

It is an interesting dynamic to observe, but to move your Digital Transformation forward in a meaningful way, these dynamics must be recognized and addressed. It does not take much: open and honest communication goes a long way toward building an effective relationship.

Field Notes: The Elephant in the Room

I was attending a conference where members of special-interest groups from IT and Marketing were meeting at the same venue. The organizers purposefully scheduled some common sessions; the conference was touted as a coming together of different functional areas within the business.

Marketing and IT teams are truly dependent upon each other and have a great opportunity to work collaboratively. But as the groups mingled, it was interesting how classic conflicts readily emerged, especially in organizations where people hadn't been working closely with their IT or Marketing brethren back home.

During a particularly feisty "open floor" session, where our hardy moderator started asking broad, fundamental questions to the group, predictable comments were coming from the assembly.

> *"Marketing doesn't know their requirements."*
>
> *"IT is always saying No."*
>
> *"Marketing is jumping on the latest buzzword bandwagon."*
>
> *"IT is overcomplicating things. We just need to get something done quickly."*

Half depressed, half bemused, I decided to jump into the conversation with what I thought was a constructive search for some common ground – the great potential for Marketing and IT to *help each other* by matching their strengths and weaknesses. And so, I observed (out loud) that IT is typically not very good at communicating. Boom!

Wow, I really did not expect the reaction I received. The Marketing folks roared their approval, while my IT peers vehemently protested. Some pointed discussion followed, with lots of side conversations, including at the cocktail hour leading up to the group dinner that night. I was having some fun now, especially when I learned the Marketing folks did not realize *I was from IT,* and I was throwing non-PC grenades in the middle of our roundtable session.

The following day, as we were wrapping up the meetings in our re-separated groups, the IT folks called me out on my comments. It was time to come out of my playful persona and make some thoughtful observations. I noted, for example, that IT was outnumbered two-to-one in the group, and I had chosen a populist persona to get the attention of the majority. However, I could have thrown a bomb in the other direction, by noting that Marketing typically does not understand "systems thinking" or the concept of long-term cost of ownership. That quickly calmed the IT leaders down; I made it out of the room alive.

There are a number of hard truths about how we think and act that Marketing and IT have to realize. A short list might include:

- **Communicating Value Is Hard**: On their own, IT and Marketing will struggle with the grey areas of digital thinking. Marketing should be able to communicate the ROI when the returns are soft, while IT should be able to bring a deeper understanding of technical complexity in the systems or data. The overall story of your Digital Transformation will flow better when the two groups work together.

- **Balancing "Good Enough" and "Built to Last"**: Marketing will typically be happy with quick-and-dirty solutions (although they are surprised when ongoing upkeep is more work than they thought). IT will want to ensure the solution never breaks (although they seemed to have skipped the lesson on the Law of Diminishing Returns). Both sides are right, and it takes common sense and an open mind to get the right balance.

- **Easy to Use Is Hard to Build** (and vice versa): Easy and quick to build gets results on the screen fast, but it can be a bear to use and maintain, especially when you are working with something for the first time. If you truly want to implement something that you can manage on your own, be prepared to learn some new technology.

- **Internal Resources Are Free** (that is why there is such high demand): In my opinion, this is the biggest and most misunderstood elephant in the room. *"Why can't IT do my stuff?"* Because they are busy working on other projects. *"But this project is really important and has high value."* Then you can afford to pay for some backfill resources to work on your project. The unspoken truth is that projects, requests, and bits of technology make sense when they can be created *for free*. But often, the ROI just isn't there if real money (external resources) needs to be invested.

Identifying and resolving these organizational dynamics is an incredibly important step in establishing your successful Digital Business.

Typically, the most mature components of your enterprise will be internal operations and customer-facing processes. To execute a Digital Transformation, technology advances alone will not be sufficient for success. Human relationships among your teams, unified behind a common objective, will win in the end.

Chapter 6

Smart, Connected Products

History and Context

So far, we have covered how information and technology have made significant changes in how Digital Business operates and connects. We are following the three waves of influence as described by Michael Porter: 30 years ago it was all about accounting systems (ERP) and automating internal processes; 15 years later came the introduction of the Internet, and a fundamental change in how we connect with our customers.

Now it is time for information and technology to make huge, disruptive changes in the products and services that we offer. Of course, I am talking about Smart, Connected Products – Porter's term[8] for the Internet of Things. This is the newest wave of change that information and technology has brought to business, coupled

---

[8] (Porter and Heppelmann, How Smart, Connected Products are Transforming Competition 2014)

with the maturing of the Internet, the growth of mobile platforms, and the accessibility of artificial intelligence.

For most companies, the realization that Smart, Connected Products will have a big impact on your markets, your competition, and your customers is the reason you are talking about a Digital Transformation in the first place. It is the trigger event. Digital is changing yet another core element of what it means to be a business, and it is time to think more holistically about managing the impact and optimizing the outcome.

This idea seems to have moved past the hype stage. Thankfully, we are no longer pestered by the breathlessly repeated statistics (20 billion devices connected to the internet by 2020, etc.). Every day, more companies are jumping in, especially in the industrial world, where the Internet of Things promises the biggest impact. Forward motion is terrific, but much like the early days of ERP and the Internet, there are competing standards, incomplete specifications, and oversimplified solutions. There are many terrific, exciting, innovative ideas changing business as we know it. However, it is important to realize that this component is not as mature as other Digital Business practices.

For many industrial manufacturers, the concept of connected devices on the shop floor sending telemetry back to a central controlling system is old news. Machine-to-machine (M2M) technology has been around for some time: wired into the local area network of a manufacturing plant; connecting PLCs across industry-standard architectures like SCADA; and providing the Operations team the ability to monitor, control, optimize, and automate. But M2M technology has typically been focused on internal operations; relatively few organizations have ventured into information as a product.

Of course, there are many companies that have made a go of this approach over the years. Early technology, including on-board electronics, remote communications, and centralized data management, was a bit tricky for them. The difference over the past five years has been the proliferation of electronics out in the field, a wider array of communications choices to bridge the gap to the cloud, and the explosion of cloud capabilities beyond the traditional database servers we simply moved to the Internet. We now have flexibly provisioned and scalable data management architectures, connected to advanced, yet accessible building blocks for powerful analytics. This is significant; artificial intelligence can transform products from expensive hunks of complicated machinery to self-aware and optimized components of a highly productive system. In the past, only the larger companies, with complicated (and very expensive) industrial systems had the profit margins and cash flows to support such an expense-heavy set of features for their intelligent products.

Current State – Strengths and Weaknesses

Getting Started

As you move beyond the hype stage for the Internet of Things (IoT), and start working with different product lines to identify and plan for real top-line growth, there is a clear need to ground the conversations in the concrete and understandable. A few years ago, when this was all still early-stage ideas, I might start by asking if they have ever heard of the "Internet of Things." I am still not surprised when I am greeted with blank stares or bemused expressions. When I list the common examples (typically, mentioning FitBit or Nest will do the trick), the lights start to go on, and we are past the buzzword. But how does this impact our industrial customers and markets?

The challenge is that most of our IoT understanding is limited to these consumer product examples, gathering personal data and sharing it with ourselves. It's a bit of a leap to go from "heightened self-awareness" to industrial applications. Then again, a fair number of engineering and product marketing teams have been experimenting with "skunk works" efforts, responding to customer requests, and dabbling in ideas for metrics that "kind of sound like that IoT thing." How can we identify and hook into that?

It helps to have a simple framework for IoT solutions, one that simplifies the exploratory conversation and breaks the ideas into easily understandable chunks. These IoT Building Blocks[9] have developed in a purposeful manner. Time and again, the dabblers have made progress in areas that they understand, but have come to an impasse on one of these five steps.

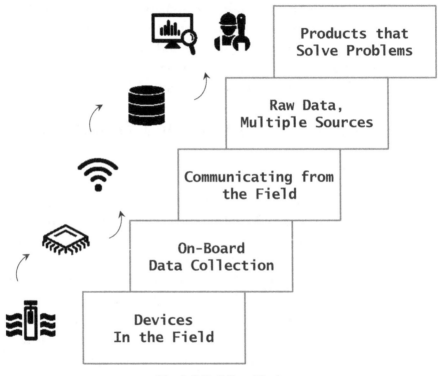

The IoT Building Blocks

Are you interested in developing a new IoT product or service? Looking for where to get started? Let us start from the bottom.

Devices in the Field: There is data to be collected, but what kind of "thing" will you be deploying? Are you thinking about adding a data component to an existing product, or developing an entirely new metering device?

---

[9] (MacLennan, A Framework for Starting the Internet of Things Conversation 2014)

On-Board Data Collection: We know what kind of data might be interesting – voltage, cycles, temperature, pressure, etc. But how exactly are you going to capture this information? What kind of measuring device, brilliant chip, or magic wire will be added, and how will you record the values?

Communicating from the Field: Assuming you can collect the information, how will you send it to the "cloud"? Are you adding a cell phone to every pump on the shop floor (maybe) or every square yard of this farmer's field (not likely)? How do you bridge that "air gap"?

Raw Data, Multiple Sources: And where exactly is this "cloud" that is receiving the data we are sending? Is it a development server in the back room, or a virtual machine running in someone else's data center? And are you locked into a classic database mentality, or will you have to contemplate unstructured data? In high volumes? From global locations?

Products that Solve Problems: Once you have picked the device, gathered the data, and stored it in a database, what is the next step? Will you develop analytics and dashboards, or just sell subscriptions to the data? And how exactly are you going to monetize this? What is the value proposition?

These five different types of challenges can launch plenty of conversations and imaginative problem solving. Thinking about these challenges using these IoT Building Blocks has proven to be very effective in getting off the mark and helping product teams make lots of interesting progress.

- Some do not know *where to start*; the IoT Building Blocks will help you gravitate to your area of expertise and make concrete progress, just to get the ball rolling.

- Some do not know *where to focus*; the IoT Building Blocks allow you to decompose the conversation and identify the biggest gap so you can get right at the toughest challenge.

- Some already have solutions for a few of these challenges, but never thought to extend their solution to become a real IoT offering. The Blocks will open their eyes to what else is possible.

- Sometimes Engineering has a great product idea, but they cannot communicate the business case. The Blocks help tee up the potential product offering in a simpler way so that Marketing folks can understand the opportunity and connect it with potential customers.

- Sometimes Marketing truly sees a great differentiator that is a response to the voice of the customer, but they cannot communicate the technical need. The IoT Building Blocks quickly identify challenge areas that Engineering will be able to target with a solution.

There are plenty of details to discuss in each of the IoT Building Blocks (lack of standards, security concerns, fast-moving technology, just to name a few). These Building Blocks are not meant to be the prescriptive path to take you from start to finish, but they will help get the conversation past the "gee whiz" stage.

Defining the Value

When introducing the idea of Smart, Connected Products, a critical early conversation concerns creating value. The focus will be different, based on your audience. A Product Manager should be thinking about how much revenue can be generated. The General Manager (or Managing Director), on the other hand, will want to hear about creating value from a broader perspective, including the entire chain of connections between yourself and your end customers. Value can be created in a number of different places, and a broader view will shed a different light on your overall digital product approach.

The diagram on the next page shows the Customer Value Chain[10]. The name refers to the macro steps between the manufacturer and the end customer – multiple participants who will be able to derive value from the information added to our products. The Customer Value Chain may be different for your organization, based on your specific path to the ultimate buyer.

---

[10] (MacLennan, IoT Field Notes: How to Identify Customer Value 2016)

IoT Features / Functions		Make It ... Manufacturer		Sell It ... Channel Partners		Use It ...	
		Prod Design	Prod Mgmt	Dealer/Distrib	OEMs	Customers	Customers' Customers
Raw Data	NPD / Proof of Concept	Input to Design	Input to Design				
	Data Feed to 3rd Party	Input to Design	Input to Design			Save Effort, Prevent Loss	Visibility
Monitoring	Notifications and Alerts	Cust Svc, Warranty	Input to Design	Service, Training	Service, Training	Save Effort, Prevent Loss	Uptime, Reliability
	Product Adoption / Usage	Cust Svc, Warranty	Mkt/Channel Performance	Revenue Growth	Revenue Growth	Prevent Loss	Return on Investment
Control	Remote Troubleshooting	Saves Effort	Input to Design	Saves Effort	Saves Effort	Predictable Performance	Uptime, Reliability
	Remote Operation	Service Revenue		Service Revenue	Service Revenue	Saves Effort	Saves Effort
Optimization	System Tuning	Service Revenue				Optimizes Performance	Promise Delivered
	Predictive Maintenance	Service Revenue		Service Revenue	Service Revenue	Save Effort, Prevent Loss	Promise Delivered
Autonomy	Data Collection, Self-Tuning		Input to Design			Optimizes Performance	Promise Delivered
	Interaction, Coordination		Input to Design	Revenue Growth	Revenue Growth	Optimizes Performance	Promise Delivered

Value is created via top line growth $\bowtie$ *(new revenue, market share), bottom line savings* $\textcircled{=}$ *(productivity, optimization)*

Customer service & loss prevention is harder to quantify – but an important part of the Value Selling conversation

For this exercise, we will keep it simple: a product manufacturer, selling to a distribution channel, with limited direct contact to the ultimate end user.

Note that Channel Partners are a critical part of the conversation, and are often the complicating factor that slows down disruptive change since there is a common (and at times legitimate) fear of disintermediation. At the very least, the channel will be wary of anything that might upset the delicate balance of forces that has evolved over the years.

Next, let's think about potential use cases. How might IoT technology be added to products? What features and functionality will be added? The diagram captures some typical applications for Things that want to connect to the Internet – stated broadly enough that they cover most IoT product ideas.

Raw Data: Early-stage efforts may focus only on data collection from products in the field to help R&D efforts. Also, some of your customers may ask only for the raw data generated from the device for their own in-house applications and analysis.

Monitoring: Tracking activity in the field, aggregating data for central visibility, and sending out alerts when there are problems.

Control: Remote configuration and operation of products in the field.

Optimization: Leveraging algorithms "in the cloud" (centrally, and separately from the point of use) to sense operations and tune the performance of devices in the field.

Autonomy: Enabling smart devices to communicate and coordinate with other devices in the same system or network of operations.

We are primarily interested in creating value that is clearly quantifiable. To keep the discussion simple, value creation will be classified as top-line growth (new revenue, increased market share) or bottom-line savings (labor productivity, asset optimization, cost-cutting, and so on).

Some businesses may find it worthwhile to call out value creation that is a bit harder to quantify; ideas like "better customer service" (which can lead to top-line growth and/or customer retention), or "loss prevention" (risk reduction, an indirect benefit that is often hard to quantify). This really depends on the audience. When arguing for investment, hard benefits are preferred. However, when having a value-selling conversation, or evaluating the strategic impact, these indirect and "soft" benefits can be well received.

The next step is straightforward, and best done with a mixed team of Customers, Engineers, and Product Managers. Think about each of the intersections on the grid as specific use cases. For each use case, capture the potential impact of your Smart Product ideas on each part of the Customer Value Chain.

Let's walk through the first row; how do features like real-time monitoring and automated notifications impact each of the links? Imagine your smart pump working away in a manufacturing facility, keeping track of its own operation and sending sensor readings back to the central database. Who might derive benefit? Working backwards:

- Smart, Connected Products will let the **end customer** know if and when maintenance is required, generating bottom-line savings by avoiding service that is not required. Unplanned downtime is reduced, even eliminated, with an early warning system that predicts bad things before they happen.

- Typically, **channel partners** provide service and training, and IoT devices that actively monitor themselves will help make sure that required service is performed (generating new revenue for the channel). These products might also let the distributor know when the operator is not using the device correctly – a nice justification for additional training. And since this information is a new and differentiating feature in the market, the dealer channel will see incremental sales due to growing market share as Smart, Connected Products are preferred over their unconnected competition.

- There is plenty of value for the **manufacturer** as well. In addition to incremental revenue for unit sales, the Product Management teams will benefit. Engineering will see live data from devices in the field, and develop a deeper understanding of operational characteristics and areas for improvement (including areas to take cost out of overengineered products). And Channel Management folks will be able to quantify things like product pull-through and territory saturation.

There is a story to be told for every row and cell in the grid. It frames the conversation, so Marketing and Engineering teams can add a wee bit of structure to your brainstorming.

Note that the structure of your Customer Value Chain – the ultimate path to your customer – can have a significant impact on this conversation. A distributor might think they are "just the middleman" with no leverage to turn on their information flows. How could they convince the OEM to participate?

The distributor developed a service offering that monitored status, sent pre-emptive communications (email or text) that included handy links to automatically order the correct replacement parts, and scheduled a service call where required. In the end, this was not just a simple revenue generator. These Smart, Connected Products helped control the OEM's market share loss in replacement parts (a very profitable line of business).

By understanding the Customer Value Chain, and the different points where value might be created, Product Managers can brainstorm their way to breakthrough ideas.

The Link to Digital Business

Products are an important component of the strategic Digital conversation within your business. The key is to pick out the critical bits that will have an impact on your customers and your markets – things like machine learning and predictive analytics, where data and statistics are changing the nature of our products and how we deliver value to our customers.

Remember, we have been talking about five components that interact and leverage each other to become a truly unified Digital Business. So how does the Internet of Things work together with everyone else?

Internal Operations

As you start your first experiments with sensors, communications, and data, take the opportunity to experiment in your own manufacturing and operational processes; why not learn, fail, iterate, and improve in private? There are many devils in the technical details, and your deep experience will be built upon the mountain of mistakes you will make. Better to keep your learning process away from the prying eyes of your eventual customers. This is a real advantage that traditional enterprises have over startup companies, who must learn and develop in the public domain.

But the real value created here is data integration. Product teams will see the value in connecting serial numbers on IoT-enabled devices with the product life cycle data coming out of your ERP: when was it manufactured, what is in the bill of materials, to whom was it sold and shipped. The ability to see and understand the life cycle and complete pedigree of a product in the field will be invaluable.

Customer Relationships

The data coming from your Smart, Connected Products will shine further light on the entire value chain – from manufacturer to distributor to end-user. All participants in that chain will get value from visibility. Product performance and utilization will be open to all, intermediaries will see future demand more clearly, and improved products and services will make those customer relationships "stickier." Smart Products will know a lot about themselves and where they came from, and everyone in the value chain (product management, engineering, distribution, and end customer) will value that complete pedigree.

Leveraging Information

Yes, there is currently a talent shortage for data scientists, but the concepts and tools are much more accessible thanks to advances in support of the Internet of Things. Smart companies, however, will not stop at their products. They will apply predictive techniques to the data coming out of their customer-facing and internal operational systems to make smarter decisions and think more proactively in both of those areas.

The Disruptive Truth

The biggest impact, however, that this component will have on your Digital Business will be increased awareness in the power of disruption. We saw it happening with the advent of the Internet, when stable markets and established businesses like newspapers and bookstores were wildly disrupted because of fundamental changes in the nature of the distribution of information to end consumers. Now that we have entered the age of the Internet of Things, this disruption is reaching into other, more traditional industries.

The hype around the Internet of Things is amazing, yet there are still plenty of folks who have not heard the term. Most will show a flash of recognition when discussing fitness trackers, smart locomotives and other images from mainstream television ads. But for many manufacturing firms, the IoT is still far away; possibly someone is dabbling in the Product Development group, but nothing concrete.

The challenge is that ideas like "smart devices" and a "connected world" are getting attention for really big, sexy implementations on high-priced equipment like tractors and locomotives, or mass marketed products that target either millions of consumers with low price and high volume, or high-end, status-based consumers based on exclusivity and look/feel.

So where does that leave specialty and industrial manufacturers? Based on the current level of buzzword hype, more manufacturers are destined to teach their IoT "Things" to collect data and send it home for analysis or join in a local conversation with other Things (now that they have something to talk about). It also seems apparent that we are all destined to do this – or else it will be done to us, via the promise (or threat) of Disruption.

But reality for most manufacturing companies has major challenges, because they are not making Highly Valuable Things or Mass-Market Things, but Specialty Things. These are industrial products with lower volumes, or niche products with very targeted appeal. And, for most manufacturing organizations, "Information as a Product/Service" will be a radical departure, as multiple groups will struggle with the change.

Product Development: We are aware of the opportunities, but detailed questions remain around metering, data transmission, data storage, and creating end products (data, analytics, services). It is still relatively early – component cost and supply can vary, and standards are still being set. And while many engineering groups are clever enough to meter products in the field, few have the same depth of experience in data transmission, storage, security, and analytics.

Operations: We have spent years buying raw materials and converting them to parts, devices, and systems while driving out cost and improving quality and service. Development, sourcing, manufacturing, and distribution of data involves a fundamentally different way of thinking and doing; this will be an interesting organizational challenge.

Product Management: The great promise, of course, is to create organic revenue growth that is scalable, sustainable, and delivers the appropriate margins. The challenge for Sales and Marketing will be to divert some of their attention to products and services that are unlike most of what they have sold in the past. Yes, there are parallels with Aftermarket and Maintenance & Service, but analytics or data subscriptions may be sold to a different functional area within the customer's organization.

So the opportunity is known, and the challenges are there. How can manufacturing companies make this happen? It is fun (and a little scary) to think of how much within your business such a disruption could change; better to think about it seriously, so you can focus on the fun and minimize the scary. When disruption becomes an active part of your Digital Business, you will think about it all the time (and that is a healthy move).

Organization and People

Information-based products and services are typically the newest component of your Digital Business – the dynamic idea or initiative (or market threat, or customer request) that really shakes things up and makes your New Product Development team stop and take notice of the changes in the landscape. This can be viewed as an exciting time for some people and an existential threat for others, as the technical skills, domain knowledge, and market understanding that brought them to this point in their career feel like they are no longer valuable.

There is a consistent pattern with product teams in established industrial companies. These folks have a deep understanding of what it means to design, market, and sell physical products that solve specific, complex problems for their customers. But when the conversation turns to contributing to earnings with "Information as a Product or Service," there is real angst in the air when we get to the simple specifics: *"Where exactly are we going to make money here –and how much? What is the 'size of the prize'?"*

Some may feel angst over the prospect while others will revel in this challenge. There is a reason these people are good at what they do – this is the *exciting* part of their job, where they make commitments on Revenue and Return! Throughout the organization, the entire Product Line team (Engineering, Operations, Marketing, Sales) feel the same level of commitment. And it is important to point out that this is typically just the beginning of the conversation – the dance between initiating the cost (by starting a build project) and delivering the benefit (by recording sales).

Still, the idea of a Digital Transformation for your products is a significantly new way of thinking for many industries; patterns that feel natural for consumer products, for example, will not make sense for industrial manufacturers and other B2B companies. There is a great leap from making and shipping mechanical stuff to providing and supporting data-enabled stuff. This leap will introduce major changes in how products and services are created and supplied to your customers. Is there also a huge change in the way you monetize those products and services?

The answer is yes and no. Most of the revenue models are familiar to manufacturers that provide aftermarket parts and service to their customers, or introduce product line extensions into existing markets and near adjacencies. Some of these revenue models include:

- **New Product**: Digital devices and software are new products, new SKUs to be added to the customer invoice. This might mean completely new finished goods, or options that can be added to an existing product. To figure out the return, Marketing will need to determine a unit price and estimate incremental sales in units.

- **Next Generation**: As an alternative scenario for the add-ons, instead of offering as an option, make the data-enabled capability a new standard feature. This would address the challenges of SKU proliferation and complexity, and reduce the problem of cannibalizing sales from other SKUs.

- **Retrofit**: Will Engineering be able to design something that can be added on as an in-field upgrade to the installed base? Depending on technical complexity, this may be an important challenge for the product engineers to solve, and an arguably easier source of revenue since we are strengthening our relationship with established customers.

Note that the ideas to this point are all one-time revenue, very much in line with the way manufacturers see ourselves; we make and sell physical products. But what about the idea of Information as a Service? Like aftermarket parts and maintenance & service contracts, this digital revenue comes in less discreetly (x units, y price, z delivery date) and more continuously (x units @ y price per month). Unit price decreases, but the volume increases, with all the benefits of recurring revenue (less bumpy, more predictable, better forecast).

- **Service Subscription**: Data, reports, analytics, and proactive product maintenance can all be delivered as part of a monthly fee-for-service model.

- **Analytics Services**: What if the data is very specific to your particular piece of equipment? Should end users or the distribution channel be expected to understand the domain as completely as your engineers? What if you made your product experts available to look at the customers' data details and provide consulting and guidance on the best way to use the equipment?

The introduction of digital Products will impact the macro environment of your products and services in other ways. Your New Product Development teams will see other changes during this transition:

- **A Bigger Pie (and Slice Thereof)**: How will adding data to your product offering change the market? When developing the marketing plan and justifying the cost/benefit model, it will be important to understand what you are proposing to do to the market. Will you simply take share from the competition with your superior product offering, now bundled with differentiating services? Or will you increase the size of the addressable market by adding new products, new services, or by entering new geographies and/or verticals?

- **Incremental Innovation**: You might be tempted to look at an information-enabled product line as simply the next generation of product development – this year's latest feature. This is a conservative approach, and overlooks the potential for changing the game in your industry. It is a valid move, but a bit too conservative for some, and not the most common approach.

- **A Bigger Data Eco-System**: Some vertical markets already have major OEM players developing data-enabled environments that your company may explore. In Agriculture, for example, equipment manufacturers like Case International and John Deere are making moves to information-enable farmers. Are they the only game in town? Clearly not – other major Ag players like Monsanto are making moves in this area as well. You may need to pick one of the major players in your industry, or try to hook into many alternatives, instead of striking out on your own.

Note that these revenue plans and market impacts are not separate and distinct – information-based products and services can be introduced using a number of these ideas.

Technology changes that enable digital products are, quite frankly, the simplest part of the changes happening to your New Product Development teams. Yes, they clearly own this component of your Digital Business, but you must realize that this is the component going through the highest amount of significant change in the very short-term. Product Line Managers and Engineers will make significant contributions to your Digital Transformation, but they will also need the support of their peers.

Field Notes: The Subtle Power of Design

The introduction of information as a new and differentiating feature in your products will draw out some surprising insights for engineers as you interact with customers trying to understand these new capabilities. Let us go back to that Creating Value graphic from a bit earlier and look a little closer.

When I first used this diagram to illustrate this part of the journey, it really helped people get the idea. But the more interesting reactions were focused on the actual illustration. Specifically, I was peppered with questions on the graphic design elements. What was the original story I was trying to tell? Who was the audience, and what was going through my head as I made the design choices?

Those are tough questions to answer, partially because this image was originally created for a different conversation, but primarily because many design decisions are made "in the moment." Still, there are a few elements that stand out in my memory – things that I believe are critically important when communicating a significant shift in thinking.

Know your Audience

Originally created for an executive audience who are used to seeing dense PowerPoint slides, this chart was filled with lots of information. It is fascinating – executives do not want to see a large number of separate slides, so the answer (apparently) is to put a lot of information into a small number of pages[11].

I have always thought that the world uses the wrong medium when we communicate dense information by PowerPoint. Why not use a Word document, a white paper or case study? And why 11 x 8.5 instead of 8.5 x 11? Landscape format might be suited for big screens and tablets, but people invariably still want to print things out. Nevertheless, a PowerPoint deck is customary and expected,

---

[11] Actually, they really just want to hear the most pertinent information, laid out succinctly. But that is a topic for another conversation...

and so, instead of building a series of pictures to tell the story, my version is all in a single table.

Make It...		Sell It...		Use It...	
Manufacturer		*Channel Partners*		*Customers*	*Customers' Customers*
Prod Design	*Prod Mgmt*	*Dealer/Distrib*	*OEMs*		
Input to Design	Input to Design				
		Service, Training	Service, Training	Save Effort, Prevent Loss	Visibility
Cust Svc, Warranty	Input to Design	Service, Training	Service, Training	Save Effort, Prevent Loss	Uptime, Reliability
Cust Svc, Warranty	Mkt/Channel Performance	Revenue Growth	Revenue Growth	Prevent Loss	Return on Investment
Saves Effort	Input to Design	Saves Effort	Saves Effort	Predictable Performance	Uptime, Reliability
Service Revenue		Service Revenue	Service Revenue	Saves Effort	Saves Effort
Service Revenue				Optimizes Performance	Promise Delivered
Service Revenue		Service Revenue	Service Revenue	Save Effort, Prevent Loss	Promise Delivered
	Input to Design			Optimizes Performance	Promise Delivered
	Input to Design	Revenue Growth	Revenue Growth	Optimizes Performance	Promise Delivered

...ue, market share), bottom line savings (productivity, optimization)
...antify – but an important part of the Value Selling conversation

Customer Value Chain (detail)

Information Structures the Picture

The table tells the story of value created along the way, from manufacturer to end customer. Typically, the Value Chain is drawn horizontally, with fancy little chevrons making up the links. However, the slide started getting visually busy. Four different use cases, four copies of the Value Chain, four sets of angles to confuse the eye... ick. I switched to simple rows of blocks – and since I like consistency, symmetry, and control, I built a table.

I am a big fan of Edward Tufte[12], and I like making use of as much ink on the page as I can, leaving behind only what is truly

---

[12] Tufte is a leading thinker in the area of effective visual communications and communication design. He has published an

required to get the point across. Simple shapes with consistent dimensions are much easier to read. And note how I delineate the rows by a lack of color, not a solid border. Negative space can be your subtle friend.

A Picture Tells A Thousand Words

Some people learn by reading, some learn by hearing, some by seeing, others by doing. I wanted to add another dimension, differentiating between top- and bottom-line benefits, but there was enough text already. A few icons help illustrate the idea, simply and cleanly – and a repeating icon does not seem as intrusive as a repeating set of text.

Reflecting back on the "mechanical" aspects of communication can be an enlightening exercise. When done thoughtfully, you should see elements of design thinking starting to show up. It is not about subjective opinions of what looks good, but a thoughtful and purposeful use of all the tools at your disposal to make change happen.

The case above was a mindful exercise to change a single reader's understanding of a story. But Design Thinking, and thinking about design, can have a big impact on any change management effort.

---

excellent series of books on visual explanations – highly recommended! (Tufte n.d.)

Chapter 7

The Data Value Chain

History and Context

The next core component of your Digital Business is Data – the bits and bytes generated by the first three components of your Digital Business. Think of the data that is created and collected by your internal operations, your customer connections, and your products in the field. It's not just the basic data management of all these sources that moves the digital needle; it is the *integration* of that data, and the creation of valuable information, across the different silos.

Skills and techniques for data integration are typically found in the people that work in Operations. This is usually the most mature digital component of any business, and these teams have developed a wide range of tools and techniques for integrating data. Now add in the customer teams, with an ability to deftly handle large volumes of unstructured data. To complete the picture, bring in data streaming from your installed products to add detail and volume. A thoughtful business will be well positioned to leverage the data in many ways, to the benefit of multiple business stakeholders.

- Order history, quality, and service wins and losses, even shipping details from your internal operations, feed the complete picture of the relationship between a customer and your company.

- Website traffic and visitor behavior, along with quotes and proposals from CRM systems, provide valuable demand planning signals to internal supply chain planners.

- Telemetry data from smart products in the field provide utilization and performance data for sales, marketing, and other customer-facing activities.

- Telemetry data from the field, combined with manufacturing details from Operations, and Distribution, and facts and figures about Sales from customer-facing systems, can provide customers with a very thorough pedigree of the products they have installed.

On top of that, there is ever-growing demand to mine this raw data for valuable information that provides insights into operations, the needs of critical customers, and the performance of products. The true challenge for many organizations is understanding the processes required to pull this information from the data, and finding the right hands for the task.

Seven Links in the Data Value Chain

Most of us are familiar with the processes required to pull information out of data. Think of them as links in the Data Value Chain – a series of unique and distinctive processes and skill sets that are required at different steps in the journey. There are seven separate and distinct processes, and seven separate roles to understand.

Insight: The first step introduces the Business Analyst – an individual who can capably navigate the tools and processes of data analysis. Of greater importance, this person should have solid experience and a deep understanding of your particular business. These are the folks who know the interesting questions; they will also understand the data required to build comprehensive answers to these questions.

Architect: This is a slightly more technical role – this person will define how to structure the required data in ways that can be sourced, collected, stored, and presented to make the analyst's job manageable.

Generate: Data collection gets real here; this step is all about pulling the actual data from our sources. Connections will be made to internal and external systems that are predictable and known. In addition, connections will be made with alternate sources, adding new and different data to the mix.

Store: We cannot skip over the need to engineer the storage and management of the data, especially when volumes get large. Cloud storage has made this step faster to implement and cheaper to operate, but it still requires intelligent engineering to maintain performance levels and keep costs managed while maintaining secure control.

Process: Now that we have collected all this data, it is time to scrub, match, normalize, and augment the facts that are known. At this point in the process you can improve on the grunt work of data processing with new and powerful technologies such as machine learning. This is the critical step – preparing the raw data and enabling new and different correlations in the streams of raw facts.

Analysis: Next, it is time for the domain experts to come back to the table to do their analysis. They are looking for patterns in the data, answering the original questions while remaining curious, looking for new and different questions that may pop up as we drill into the details.

Present: The final, most important step in the process is typically the least appreciated. A different set of skills is required to present results and develop helpful visualizations in a dynamic way. It is not enough for our analyst to be able to see the patterns and draw the conclusions. She must find ways to make it understandable to the other decision-makers who are relying on these insights.

A Mix of Skills

As you travel along the Data Value Chain, consider the broad mix of skills required to do each one of those steps. These range from the softer, design-oriented, inspirational and artistic skills required for insights and analytics; to the precise, technically deep, scientific and engineering skills required to source, store, and process the data; to the curious and interpretive analysis skills that must convey our insights to the rest of the team.

This is a common path for most companies, and it is highly likely that everyone reading this book knows of someone who is a highly valuable Super Analyst, strong in four or five of these skills and passably competent in the rest. And we all know that these folks are relatively rare – so-called "purple squirrels" that organizations hoard to themselves, refusing to share contact information (and even the fact that these people exist) with peers in the industry.

It is extremely difficult to find these folks, which is why your Team can be a significant risk and a severe limitation to a scalable, sustainable Digital Business. Any process that is highly reliant on a single individual is a risk. And any organization that limits itself this way is failing to take full advantage of the data it has at its disposal. A single key individual lacks the right mix of skills to perform each of these steps in the best way possible.

A great Digital Business has to solve this problem by bringing on a blended team of individuals with the right mix of skills to cover all these steps. You cannot find it in one person; you must hire, develop, and cross-train to cover all the bases.

Where to Start

Talented teams are the biggest challenge for this component of your Digital Business. How do you staff your team with such a wide array of different skills? Some necessary skills will be straightforward – raw tech knowledge such as data structures and architectures, cloud computing, or even something as "arcane" as Data Science, an area where all can acknowledge a severe talent shortage. Fear not – there is always an opportunity to identify skilled learners, to find people who are adept at adding new knowledge and flexible in their understanding of what they know, what they do not know, and how to bridge the gap. And there is always the need for people who can deliver training and teach technical skills. It's a basic matter of time and aptitude.

But what about the softer skills – things like a sense of design, the ability to communicate with empathy, and intellectual curiosity? And how do you answer Pete's challenge? How do you recruit or train someone who can see meaningful patterns in the data noise, be able to understand it and drill down to the relevant details? How do you hire and/or train someone who can ask the *next* question?

Unfortunately, recruiting "imagineers" is not that easy. The trick here is to set up an environment in which people have the ability, the permission, and the responsibility to answer your questions and follow up with a few of their own. To be sure, this is not in the skill set of most analysts; you may have to give a little bit on some of the technical aspects of the role. Know you are probably not going to find this behavior among the best technical folks or the best report writers. Remember that you are not looking for a single person, but a combination of folks on a diverse, multi-person team.

The interview process is a great place to screen for these skills. You will need to stock up on your repertoire of open-ended and thoughtful questions that are focused on delivering relevant results and creating real value.

"How do you evaluate and quantify value to the business?"

"Tell your story of success; what does it look like, and how would you measure it?"

"What key training did you need to become 'smart'?"

"What additional training data access tools would you need to become 'smarter'?"

"How would you train your replacement?"

"How would you write a job description for this role?"

We all know people who are really great at their jobs – the "go-to" folks who always get tapped for tough tasks, hard answers, or open-ended questions. They have a certain knack, an ability to quickly understand how to deconstruct a challenge into things with which they are familiar, and a preference for action to find components to the answer and mash them together into something new.

Field Notes: What is the Real Skills Gap?

As we go through the recruiting process, experience tells us that there is one skill that is very difficult to find. How do you screen for curiosity, persistence, and creativity? How do you find *imagination*?

I recall a conversation from one of those meetings that is familiar to experienced digital professionals trying to introduce new ideas. As I tried to connect with Pete, the "old dog" president of a multibillion-dollar distribution company, I tried to appeal to his information-savvy background. Don't get me wrong – this "old dog" was hip to the power and opportunity presented by digital tools and thinking. He certainly preferred to run his business and make decisions with as much hard information as he could get his hands on. I walked into his office with the typical technology lead-in, talking about all the great dashboards we could set up for his executive team. "Just tell me what you want the screen to say," I insisted, "and I can make it happen."

Pete was not enthused about starting with a blank screen; it is always easier to edit than it is to create. And Pete even joked about the impact. "Given enough information," he said, "I will make my team miserable by asking a million questions, and being able to call them out whenever they filter the results and protect me from the truth." We had a good laugh – I knew his team, and I knew the idea of arming Pete with the details would be something less than helpful. But Pete turned our humor into a strong discussion point: "I don't want to be the only person asking questions."

Pete explained it this way: "Each day, someone comes to me with one of our standard management reports. As we review it together, I will see something that makes me think. I will ask a question about a specific number. *'Why are sales low in this region? Why is inventory up at that location? Why is on-time delivery falling for that product line?'* The manager will go off and have a think about it, find the answers to my questions, and come back the next day – or maybe even a few hours later – with another report, showing the requisite depth to answer my question.

"It's a good answer, one that specifically gets to the heart of the question I was asking… and then I will look at another area of that report, and see another anomaly, or change, or funny-looking trend, in another relevant dimension. Note that it's not always a negative – there may be positive changes, trends, or indicators to be discovered. And I will ask the next question… *why? where? when? how?* And the manager will go off and have another think about it, and return again with specific answers to my specific questions.

"And so it goes – all the while, the manager sees success and progress, because she is able to *provide the answers*. But that is not success to me. The manager should be the one to *ask the questions.*

"So that's what I need from your digital systems and processes," Pete concluded. "Build something that helps people become smarter, more curious, and more insightful. Find a training program or a tool that inspires people to develop some intellectual curiosity, that encourages people to *ask the next question.* Instead of coming into my office with answers, I'd rather have them come in with observations and questions of their own."

Wow – what a gift of trust and openness. Pete was not trying to brush me off with an impossible task; on the contrary, he was demonstrating that he really understood the possibilities of Digital Business, along with the practical realities of skills and talent. It takes a combination of important skills to transform data into information, and a set of rare and powerful aptitudes and tendencies to go from information to knowledge, action to value.

Field Notes: Training to be a Superstar

I asked one of my favorite project managers how she became that indispensable team member – the person most in demand for the important projects. "I remember when we recruited you for the IT team," I said. "You came to the table with this terrific base of knowledge. Where did you get that?"

This is an effective way to drill for an answer to a difficult, wispy question. I was not asking for theory or conjecture. I was looking for a specific example of a clearly defined success. Month over month, after she first started working with the system, how did she develop her skills? And her answer was straightforward.

"You just dive right in, and figure the answer out for yourself," she said. With most digital systems and processes, standard training is great for baseline skills – how to navigate the screens, where all of your core menu options are located, and how the basic workflows for key transactions or processes operate. But the most valuable things to learn, she pointed out, were the online help system, the knowledge base of previously answered trouble tickets, and Google.

Armed thusly, a reasonably talented person can find the answers for themselves, or find someone else who can help solve the issue. Building this extended community of experts can develop your knowledge base, collecting the myriad little details that will make up your highly valued brilliance.

At this point in the "training" process, it is either sink or swim. *You* must figure it out, because no one else will. And if you survive the first month or so, and wish to remain working in this role or on this team, you will learn – very rapidly, sometimes by rote, sometimes by inventing new knowledge.

After a few months, new hires who survive this process will have demonstrated a knack for self-directed learning, plus an interest in being known as the person who can answer questions. This leads to the next step: finding people who can generate their own questions – people who can see opportunity emerging from the funny patterns of noise in those help desk tickets, program bugs, incoming emails, water-cooler questions, and recurring problems. They can apply systems-level thinking to issues with business processes, data, or technology, and with a deep appreciation for the domain – the specifics about your customers, markets, and operations.

Yes, this training and development takes some time, but you can build an environment that promotes this type of thinking in a straightforward way. The key is to focus on problem solving with knowledge retention, working to kill root cause issues, and capturing knowledge around solutions and workarounds to avoid solving the same problems over and over again.

To be clear, this is not something you can easily automate. It takes the right kind of person, with an innate sense of curiosity, self-confidence, and some basic digital aptitude. Put that kind of person in the right environment, and you will be able to internally develop critical digital talent that is desperately sought after in the marketplace.

Chapter 8

Enabling Your Team

History and Context

So far, we have talked about the obvious digital components of your Digital Business – systems and processes that support internal operations, bring us closer to our customers, and change the nature of our products. We have discussed the critical connective tissue – data – and the skills required to extract information to create real value. But what is the one thing that's missing – the one thing that makes all of this work?

It may be a surprise, but the answer is decidedly non-digital; it's all about *people*. Specifically, it is about your employees and teams who execute your internal processes, connect with your customers and distributors, and build and service your product offering. To truly excel in a Digital Business, your internal team must be present, participating, and truly engaged.

Simply declaring a Digital Transformation will not address current challenges. If you currently struggle with siloed information, closely held by your operations, marketing, and engineering teams, you will still have to address the challenges that silos present. Why would those walls automatically come tumbling down? They were built by people, and people are still in these organizational and behavioral structures.

However, your employees may be ahead of you, waiting patiently for the signal to change. Has your team makeup shifted in the past few years? You may be building up a team of digital natives already, attracting people who are expecting to work with business information in a different way in much the same way as they digitally immerse themselves in their personal lives.

The Power of Engaged Teams

Time marches on, and the mix of employees in different generational cohorts is always changing. Pew Research has looked at the mix[13] of Millennials, Gen Xers, and Baby Boomers in the workforce. Each of these generations is roughly one-third of your workforce, but 2016 was the first year that Millennials became the largest generational cohort in the mix.

There are important differences in the way these groups think digitally. For example, Baby Boomers are quite comfortable communicating with email, and have developed years of important manners and customs that are expected of people that are "good communicators." Millennials, on the other hand, prefer different tools and methods to make their connections, with different styles, expectations, and implicit assumptions. Neither camp is incorrect; communication in any media is a nuanced and changing thing. But as the overall mix evolves, your team is clearly shifting to a more digitally savvy and assumptive population.

This growing group of workers also thinks differently about the kind of company they prefer. Much is being written about Employee Engagement[14], the idea that the degree to which

---

[13] (Fry 2018)

[14] (Edmans 2016)

employees are engaged (i.e. they understand the company's role and vision, get the support they need from their managers, and have the required resources to succeed in their job) is very important to them personally, and directly related to the success of the business.

Of course, it does not take much effort to find contrary opinions[15]. Some will not agree with 100 percent of the pro-Engagement arguments, while others see Employee Engagement as real and quite valuable; it just makes sense.

Collaboration in Practice

Working within a team, and really opening up to each other to collaborate in an open and trustful way, is not easy. Have you ever been in one of these situations? ...

---

[15] (Garrad and Chamarro-Premuzic 2016)

Field Notes: One for Practice

A large project was looming, and the leadership finally wanted to dive in headfirst. A recent (we will call it NewCo) and very large (30 percent of our combined revenues) acquisition needed to be integrated into our supply chain and distribution network. Customers were demanding it, but we had spent the first nine months after the acquisition maintaining the status quo, acting like two separate companies. The shareholders, our customers, and our employees knew we were leaving an awful lot of value on the table by not moving forward.

There were a few theories behind a take-it-slow approach. "Cultural sensitivity" was lauded as an important reason to proceed carefully, but part of our collective pause was *fear of the unknown*. True, NewCo was stable and strong, with mature systems for internal operations. But like all gargantuan projects, the original ERP implementation at our company had its fair share of headaches – big problems that stay with you through the years. And since the original Big Project, our core team had scattered; some had taken on other tasks in IT, some had gone into non-IT roles, and many had moved on to other employers.

Still, time was passing, and even the most pessimistic among us felt the costly challenge of trying to live on two systems. It was time to grab a mitt and get in the game!

Now Things Get Interesting

The executive team, eager for action and finally ready to make some of the tougher organization and culture decisions, was starting to pay attention to the confident people planning the integration. They knew the Operations team, armed with established processes, could handle the increased volume that NewCo would bring. The more we looked at ourselves, the more we saw talented, knowledgeable people pushing billions in revenue through a complex distribution network while keeping customer deliveries on-time and inventories low.

All true, but this consistency was delivered in an environment of slow, steady, incremental growth – not a 30 percent burst in demand. And unfortunately, some overconfidence started creeping in. "How tough could it be," some asked, "since many from the Old Team are still working here? We can pull together a team and whip this thing together in a couple of weeks... no problem."

At first, they did not listen to the important facts. The last big internal go-live for the team was at least six years prior, and the knowledge had started to fade. Some of the old team was gone, and that tight-knit, collaborative style of working had faded from disuse. In addition, this new acquisition had seven locations, and the largest single go-live weekend from our past was three locations. We had to face facts. We were talking about putting together a team to address a hugely different challenge, with a skeleton crew from our previous successes.

Thankfully, the company had made another acquisition a year earlier. This was an easier bite to take – 30 percent of the size of NewCo, and only two locations (building #2 being a little distribution warehouse across town). We decided to convert this smaller company first to give ourselves an opportunity to dust off the cobwebs and practice before the eventual Big Project.

In hindsight, this was a terrific idea because we ran into plenty of problems. Nothing major in the technical areas, but the project struggled mightily from decentralized issue tracking, inconsistent on-the-floor support, nuanced accounting changes that were not contemplated in the original rollout, and no detailed hour-by-hour plan for the all-important go-live weekend.

The implementation barely made it through, and limped over the finish line as a qualified success. One might think of it as a failure, but the leadership team saw it as a great success. This smaller project ended up being a strategic success because we re-learned a lot of the tasks, behaviors, processes, and communication links that we had forgotten. If we had not completed the smaller project for practice, the larger undertaking would have been a catastrophic failure, causing significant problems for our customers.

Like Riding a Bicycle

It's not just the project team that benefited from doing the smaller project first. When we finished it, there were plenty of people smarting from the painful experience we had just endured. It was widely recognized that the ERP conversion was not optional, but we very mindfully applied the learnings from the recently completed lead-in effort to avoid major communications and planning issues that would have massively delayed the bigger and much more complex implementation.

The larger implementation turned out to be one of the best go-lives the company had ever experienced. Customers barely knew we were making the change; that is a great success metric for a project team.

Build One to Throw Away

Build One to Throw Away is a pattern that appears in many places; test markets for new products, iterative development for websites and reports, even pre-season football games. When you are trying to introduce wildly new or risky work to your organization, a pilot program is a terrific way to get folks comfortable with the impending change. And if the team seems a bit too enthusiastic about approving that big project budget on process or technology that is very new, a proof of concept phase will allow the group to see real-world results while reducing the risk and cost of major failure.

Large projects introducing product and process innovations for your customers will often involve components that represent some risk.

New Technology: Has your team ever worked with this specific technology before? Skills learned on one platform do not always transfer well to other platforms. Modern web development is getting more advanced every day, and mobile development requires a very different set of tech competencies. As the Internet of Things comes along, the ground shifts again.

New Processes: It is a reasonably safe bet that business process and tech capability have changed a lot in the past five years, enough to suggest that old assumptions, skills, and experience have a good chance of failing and should be dealt with carefully.

New Teams: The people with the required skills have moved on to different roles. If the original team captured significant knowledge, now it is time to transfer it. If not, you will have to teach a new crew from scratch.

New Environment: You may not know all the rules; the world changes every year, and your old assumptions may not hold true. This goes for internal projects (facilities relocations, major systems upgrades, etc.) just as much as the external ones (websites, product launches, etc.)

Field Notes: Fighting over Amber Boxes

Change is a natural part of the Digital Transformation process and nothing to worry about, as long as you do not get too caught up in the drama of your preferred point of view. Remember the last time you brought a multi-function team together with the charge to "think different"?

I can recall the interesting parts of the conversation quite clearly; I'm standing at the whiteboard, leading a technical ~~disagreement~~ discussion about a particular data conversion component in a macro environment of sensors and data, hardware and software. This type of discussion pops up many times during the introduction and incorporation of innovations; we were debating definitions and abstract concepts, technical specifics, data volumes, and vendor pedigrees. And we were starting to burn time on the schedule until someone stepped back and noticed how hard we were arguing over a couple of amber boxes drawn on a whiteboard.

The sketch in question was a "conceptual architecture" for a new IoT product; an abstraction created solely to illustrate a point to a globally, technically, and motivationally diverse team. This architecture would eventually provide building blocks for multiple Internet of Things products; it was a valuable document that aimed to make our lives easier. So why all the angst?

Looking back, it would have helped to refocus on the objective; we were trying to get the whole team to 1) agree on the problem definition, and 2) directionally align for a problem solution. It was fairly broad success criteria, and not so specific that it required a 20-page, detailed tech spec with a full budget and build plan. But the conversation had shifted to a parsing contest, with shades of meaning mixed with design and tech egos. The conversation was not so aggressive, but was definitely hampered by the participants' high confidence in what they knew, along with a comfortable assumption that the world outside their experience bubble carried little value.

Could we benefit from a do-over, and try to reconvene for another discussion? Of course – we are the existential makers of our own experience, and this is classic change management material. An open discussion over digital differences helps, a simple reminder that it's not important to be right in every debate...

✓ You may be wrong.

✓ You may be blindered.

✓ You may be unintelligible.

Ah – that last one, by the way, is often the real issue. Communicating complexity, searching for concrete words for abstract ideas, explaining the innovative New to those deeply invested in the established Old – words can be terrifically tricky things.

So what does success look like? And what did we need to do to bring the team back together?

Victory #1 – Get the team on same page

- Be prepared to speak in words, pictures, stories, and examples.

- Make sure the team is not using similar words to mean *different* things.

- Make sure the team is not using different words to mean *similar* things.

Victory #2 – Get the team moving in the same direction

- Now that you have defined, discussed, and debated the As-Is and the To-Be, focus on the path to get there.

- The first-step specifics are important, but you do not need the entire illuminated path to agree on the next step. We are trying to overcome organizational inertia, and action brings answers.

The Link to Digital Business

Simply put, a Digital Business cannot succeed unless it knows how to connect with people, and your employees are the ones who will do the connecting! You can and must dig a little deeper here and focus on building and leading great teams that can drive ideas around human factors, engineering, and design thinking.

As we have noted before, all components of digital strategy share energy with each other, and our teams are no different. There are ways to measure and manage intangible things like Employee Engagement with meaningful metrics that focus on the intent of the program. Design Thinking is one of many challenging skill sets that has to be shared across the different teams – not just with the creatives in Marketing or the product designers in Engineering. Everyone needs to understand this new way of thinking.

Pay attention to teams – engaged, focused teams – and how they incorporate into your Digital Business. The way you build and grow teams capable of surviving and thriving in a fast-changing digital environment is going to be the very non-technical, analog differentiator between organizations whose digital strategies drive the business forward, and those that fall to the wayside.

Why Should I Care?

Change is rarely easy. Some debate for hours the depth of their angst before getting started; others shift with the wind, grudgingly accepting a bit of backtracking near the end. But change is a natural part of the process and nothing to worry about as long as you don't get caught up in the drama of your preferred point of view.

Introducing wild new ideas takes a bit of thought. If you want to get someone's attention on a topic that appears to come in from left field, put it in a reasonable context.

Take Digital Products, as an example – a widely talked about mega-trend promising to overrun the world with acquisitive, connected, and chatty devices. Many are jumping on the bandwagon. The topic is getting lots of play in engineering labs, customer conversations, and the executive wing. We are also seeing some maturation of thought, and voices from different industries are laying out their own versions of a similar story. But do not dismiss these vertical analyses as derivative. It is important to put new ideas into context, and to give your team a reason to devote some of their precious attention by laying out the imperative: why should we care?

A good first step is to clarify which end of the Income Statement has your focus. Are we talking about Top Line or Bottom Line?

Cost Savings and Operational Efficiency: For some organizations, IoT technology promises to drive efficiency along the entire Supply Chain. Cheap, everywhere monitoring can enable data-driven optimization of the plant floor, the distribution channel, even the end-user service arm of your business. You are a *consumer* of IoT technology; point-of-use tech is typically inexpensive, and your value comes from adding domain expertise to target the biggest areas of opportunity.

Revenue Growth: Other businesses will create value by adding information to their products. In reality, they are changing the nature of their offering, from manufacturing and selling widgets to fulfilling a specific job for the customer. You are a *creator* of IoT technology, applying existing tools, but remixing into a new value proposition for end customers (and profitable top-line growth).

Clarifying true focus on what you are trying to achieve does wonders, but do not limit yourself to the "easy out" of cost savings. Sustainable revenue growth is the kind of value creation that ownership really needs – a great opportunity to move the needle.

Strategic Impact

This focus on the bottom line can be helpful, but it may not be enough to sway the powers that be. Why should IoT be any different from the multitude of past data-based advancements (data acquisition, RFID, e-commerce, CRM, etc.)?

Information as a Feature: In many industrial markets, incumbent vendors enjoy stable market share due to high switching costs; it's just easier to stick with the established solution. That is great for your baseline revenue, but growth into adjacent markets is very difficult. Information becomes a new, compelling feature that overcomes market inertia and high switching costs; value does not come from the information directly, but from incremental share gain for core products.

Information as a Strategic Weapon: The real promise of gathering lots of data is the application of Artificial Intelligence to look for signals amidst the noise. The tools and techniques are quickly coming down to earth, and it's not rocket science anymore. Applied correctly, with the right amount of domain expertise to guide the models, AI can provide organizations with information to develop actionable insights. Predictive Maintenance? How about Predictive *Investments* in applied technologies, vertical niches, or geographies?

Open your mind and think big, but when talking with the decision makers, make sure your "big ideas" connect with their understanding of the forces that make and move the markets in which you operate.

Big ideas are great, but the real magic is progressing from idea to implementation. New ways of thinking will affect people, processes, and technology in your organization, and you will need to work through these topics in that order. Change is typically met with a wary eye, especially when incumbent thought leaders feel that things are well-established and under control. The transformative change implied with digital strategies for products and operations may appear daunting. Start the journey with a clear vision of the possible, in a context where teams can see their success.

Chapter 9

Accelerating Your Digital Transformation

Seeing the Signs – Has It Already Begun?

For some organizations, there can be a palpable excitement in the air when talk turns to all things digital. You may find that many folks in the organization want to become a Digital Business, and are actively advocating for such a pivot. Why? Because in a very real way, we have all become digital individuals; data and technology have permeated our lives through consumer tools, products, and services. The expectations we have developed in the world of personal technology are translating directly to our business experiences.

- We want systems and processes that automate internal operations to function as easily and smoothly as our favorite apps and websites.

- We rail against the usability and cost of internally delivered corporate technology when we are so used to highly functional apps on our smartphones that we can install "for free."

- We expect all our enterprise systems, projects, and analysis tools to be inexpensive and easy to implement. *"Why does it cost so much to build something new, when I can get it online so cheaply?"*

Another early indicator of a business already thinking about "becoming Digital" occurs when people start to talk about internal processes, customer relationships, and products in terms usually associated with consumer digital concepts. Ask the lunchroom crowd about their favorite smartphone apps, and they will launch into deep and knowledgeable conversations about how Amazon Prime, Waze, and Google Translate have transformed their customer journeys over the years.

Decentralized Tech and "Shadow IT"

Decentralized decisions about the application of Digital tools and processes is a growing trend, pushing decision making and investments closer to the customer. This can be a powerful change when done well, as different areas of the business bring innovative, high-value idea capabilities to better serve their customers, create a great company, and create value for the owners.

When you take a step back, it is clear that Information and Technology already permeate your business. Often referred to as "shadow IT," this rambling inventory of unsustainable technology assets can be a frustration for IT or Finance managers. But these are not frivolous or "fun" systems; the range (and inherent importance) of investment and functionality is broad and fascinating.

Finance: This team is a heavy user of consolidation and reporting tools, with their own collection of super users, data analysts, and information designers. It is fascinating that so much of corporate America runs on spreadsheets, some of which are amazing in their sophistication and complexity. These are truly custom software developments – complex systems in their own right, and completely owned by the Finance team.

Sales & Marketing: Most website projects, from brochureware to e-commerce, are conceived, budgeted, and run by the folks from Marketing (typically with external tech help). It's the same with Sales organizations and their CRM systems that are delivered either on-premise or via the cloud (aka Software-as-a-Service), with systems typically selected, justified, developed, and administered within the Sales department, separate from other enterprise data.

Operations: Operations is a primary consumer of ERP systems when it comes to planning, purchasing, manufacturing, and transportation. Operations will also have their share of savvy technologists who are looking at material handling systems, sensors for operational efficiencies, and highly automated manufacturing machines (which also need to connect via the Internet to their OEM masters). You may also see this team bringing in handhelds and other devices to simplify the tasks on the floor without sacrificing transactional discipline and data accuracy.

Product Development: Engineering teams are long-time users of the most complex and expensive workstations in the building, driving some fascinating and sophisticated design and build software. Engineering has often been the group that wants full control over their corner of the network, demanding the highest horsepower machines to drive their complex 3D models. In many businesses, Engineers are the ones buying the cutting-edge 3D printers and learning new design skills. As sensors, firmware, and data become part of your business' products and services, we are seeing software developers (firmware, web apps, analytics, data science) added to the Product Development team.

Human Resources: This is another important set of technology users who rely on systems from the mundane to the highly strategic, including payroll, Performance Management, and Talent Management systems that ensure the future of the organization.

This is another functional area that benefits from advancements in SaaS offerings, recruiting, and training and development.

IT: The team traditionally responsible for "keeping the trains running," IT manages phones, desktops, and internal networks. In most organizations, IT is also the place to look for report writers and data wranglers, communications specialists, and the deepest ERP expertise.

All of these areas are realizing localized benefits from their small corners of the digital world. However, the counter argument to the disconnected growth of digital is that it leads to duplication and fragmentation for diminishing enterprise value. Without a clear strategic vision, this technology spend of precious resources (time *and* money) devolves into a cost of doing business. These systems are typically not a differentiator for real growth, and therefore, many will see it as something that can and should be centralized.

This is not meant to be a rant against decentralization – quite the contrary. Over the years, the slow growth of shadow IT and the democratization of technology has really been a canary in the coal mine, providing the formative stages of an organization's Digital Strategy. People are using information and technology to automate internal processes, get closer to the customer, and transform products and services – all worthy goals, and the first three components of our Digital Business. But the difficulties with this disconnected approach are a common source of frustration, and include islands of automation, too many versions of the truth, a lack of integration, and a dearth of required skills. This organic and siloed growth is missing the next two components – Data and Team.

If you have a truly Digital Business mindset, the answers to these cultural challenges should not be simply an exercise in budget control. A better approach would be to understand how information and technology are used to help drive the business forward. It is not about gathering control of these resources under a single department to leverage costs. Better to drive toward answer to two important the real question: how does Digital drive the strategic objectives of the company?

The Centralized vs. Decentralized Debate

Is your organization considering, or already using, this decentralized model? Are digital resources and decisions pushed down to business units inside the company? This simplistic description masks a lot of detail because terms like *resources*, *decisions*, and *business units* mean different things to different people. But there are common threads in the discussions that lead up to this decision, and the options are not entirely black and white.

The decision to centralize or decentralize does not have to be a strictly binary choice between two bad scenarios – an authoritarian, top-down culture of control that stymies innovation, versus the "wild west" of no standards, no integrations, and no cost leverage that impede collaboration. There are pros and cons at both extremes, and like most decisions in business, the optimal truth is somewhere in the middle – a blend of the best ideas, coupled with a thoughtful effort to mitigate the inherent challenges to deliver positive results.

Resource Optimization

Typically, this conversation starts in organizations with a centralized IT function that struggles to keep up with quickly changing demands while maintaining their founding focus of systems reliability. The IT team is frustrated because they perceive cost has become the primary driver of investment priorities; it is fascinating to note how quickly IT conversations move to focus on cost control and bottom-line topics. This is why the centralized model is preferred by IT – a primary tactic is to take advantage of the organization's size to aggregate purchasing power and get better pricing.

There are strategic implications as well. Defining clear-cut standards for technology purchases and processes reduces complexity, enables predictability and reliability for core systems, facilitates integration of data and processes, and establishes an environment where collaboration and knowledge sharing can take place. Wouldn't it be better to centralize and optimize resources for these core services, freeing up time and investment in the rest of the business to focus on the customer, and drive the top line?

Point of Impact

But organizations are still looking toward decentralization as an improved model. Why? The strategic view is a recognition that this conversation is much bigger than IT. We are talking about how our business performs daily work, how we connect with our customers, and the very nature of the products and services that we provide. It's not just the bottom line; it's all about maximizing the power and value of your customers.

A successful organization puts the customer at or near the center of their focus. In this world, the optimal organization moves decision-making power as close to the customer as possible. If your focus is on your customer, you need to be agile, responsive, and able to continuously develop and enhance processes that deliver value right at the point of impact.

The more tactical view is a practical view. The organization needs or wants new things and better capabilities, but is frustrated by the costs. Why can't everything be as simple as downloading an app?

Searching for Best Practices

When contemplating a change of control for these critical functions, the first step is to realize that there are many viewpoints. Do not assume that any one team has all the answers; keep an open mind, and look for the tradeoffs.

When the topic of decentralized Digital is broached, the incumbents with stakes in the game (IT, Marketing, Product Development) need to fight the urge to assert control. You do not have to see this as a challenge to your abilities; it is a recognition that the status quo is limiting the business in some way. Look at this process as the start of a healthy conversation about the critical requirements of the business, the assumptions and risks of any decision, and a bit of discovery on best practices.

At the same time, people in the functional areas, product lines, and business units that wish to assert control and make their own decisions need to go into this with eyes wide open. Our perception of cost may need to change, since we may lose the leverage of the larger user base. And the amount of time and energy required to understand the options, implement the systems, and provide ongoing support may be a big surprise.

Impact, not Control

How to break the impasse? Look to examples from the outside. Since we are talking about digital capabilities, we can look to technical architecture for some interesting insights.

- "Mobile first" strategies point to *decentralization* – specific, limited, focused tech at the point of impact.

- Cloud concepts point to *centralization* – hugely leveraged support of infrastructure, with tons of flexibility and agility for deployment and support.

- Open source tech and Agile process will lean toward *decentralization* by empowering the end points to build bespoke solutions to address specific challenges.

None of these examples are clear-cut; you can make a contrarian case for each...

- "Mobile first" strategies point to *centralization* – delivering predictable results by defining a platform with which all apps must comply.

- Cloud concepts point to *decentralization* – providing smarter components but pushing responsibility for solution architecture out to the edge.

- Open source tech and Agile processes only work when *centralization* concepts like standard work and strictly documented process enable distributed development.

At the end of the day, the right choice is made by focusing on impact. "Aligned with our core objectives (Why), we can design the best environment and methods (How), and deliver on our commitments to the Customer (What)."

The alternative is to worry about control. "When I can direct the tasks and resources (What), I am better able to pick the methods (How) to deliver on my objectives (Why)."

The latter is upside-down; the thought process is backwards. In so many disciplines, the mantra is always to focus on the objective, the problem we are trying to solve, and the value we are trying to create. If we base our decisions on driving for the biggest impact, we will make better decisions on organization, process, and technology.

Run to the Toughest Problems

With some people in the organization, the initial conversation might go something like this ...

"Hey, let's start our next big project – Digital"!

"Well, I don't know. With every Big Project*, you can pretty much predict what's going to happen; something Bad**...

> * You know what they mean by "Big Project" – one of those highly visible, big budget affairs that will end up changing a lot of people's jobs, and take a huge chunk of people's time to get done. Big stuff, like new product launches, e-commerce web sites, ERP implementations, mergers, acquisitions, divestitures, reorganizations...
>
> ** You know what I mean by "Bad" – let's face it, we're all too busy focused on our current priorities to take on Yet Another Project. The last time someone tried this, it ended in tears, cursing, and big write-offs. And the wrong people ended up leaving the company – not the ones that screwed up, but the ones that got fed up and left.

"Hmmm ... Might as well not change a thing – the company is running well, the customers don't want us to change, the product is doing great against the competition ..."

The Unspoken Truth

Fortunately, that conversation rarely happens out loud – but unfortunately, it's going on in a lot of people's minds as the teams prepare for your Digital Transformation. We know we cannot stay on the same path indefinitely – the company runs well now, but can we scale up as demand increases? As products change?

Our customers are asking for innovation, and the competition is not standing still.

We *know* this to be true. We *wish* that it were not...

> *I have my job down to a science now, I have control over my time, the systems are stable, I can get home for dinner on time... I have other problems to worry about.*

> *Let's not mess this up – I just got that knotty problem fixed...*

Ah, but now we are drilling to the heart of the matter – the 800-lb gorilla in the room, that no one wants to acknowledge but everyone knows is there.

Spotlight on the 800-Pound Gorillas

These "Gorillas" are those critical, repeating issues that have torpedoed business changes, process improvements, and all manner of tech silver bullets for years. Everyone knows about them, but no one wants to address them or drive to any conclusions. Alternatively, everyone knows about them – they are openly discussed – but no one has been able to change them, and frankly we cannot imagine a world without them.

Concerns might include the following:

- *We have had complicated and convoluted pricing agreements for as long as I can remember. You'll never get customers to accept a simplified discount structure. It's never been done before, it's what they expect. So everything we do with pricing (approvals, changes, new contracts, e-commerce) must support this complexity.*

- *We can eliminate SKUs, simplify BOMs, and change material handling processes, but all of our processes rely on a "smart part number" that streamlines internal operations. If we change (to* system-generated part numbers), *there will be a ton of retraining required.*

- *We have complete ERP data – everything we need to know to make and ship the products. But the marketing data (everything required to catalog, present, educate, and sell via e-commerce) is kept in a million different places, and no one owns the process.*

- *It takes a lot of time to add new item numbers into the system, unless someone personally expedites through all the steps. But we've never been able to automate the workflow and streamline because no one owns the overall process. And no one wants to own the process, because it is a tedious, thankless task.*

- *There is only one person who knows how that process works and he has never documented that process. He is afraid of sharing the knowledge for fear of obsolescence.*

Run (*Sprint!*) to the Toughest Problems

Every company has a few of these major issues blocking the path to their digital future. They are real, important, and valid!

Do not jump to the conclusion that these issues are frivolous, outdated thinking, or just wrong. These are things about the company, the product, the channel, the people, that arise *precisely* because every organization is wonderful, fascinating, different, and unique. These are tough challenges that have cleverly developed their own solutions which (unfortunately) have reached a point where they no longer scale, or are not flexible enough to accommodate customers, markets, etc.

There is no easy way to fix these things, so the best time to address them is *right away.* Don't wait until you are three months into your Digital Transformation to start talking about the tough issues. Try sprinting to these issues as fast as possible. Make an outlandish statement:

Let's do the ERP implementation in three months.

Let's do the e-commerce implementation in three weeks.

Let's cut 50 percent of our SKUs this month.

Let's announce flat rate pricing this week.

Immediately, people will point out why such timelines are impossible for a number of wonderfully specific reasons. *Fantastic!* Let's work on those reasons first! Force the tough conversations, question conventional wisdom, bite the bullet on the tough stuff, and do it before the expensive consultants start charging and the fancy technology starts collecting dust.

Field Notes: Change Management

It sounds obvious, but bears repeating: Every time you launch into yet another "transformational initiative," there are two critically important success factors to focus on: Change Management and User Acceptance. Because these are such core focus areas, every experienced project manager has war stories to share. Here are a few.

Culture Is Huge

The team went through the requirements phase of a typical Knowledge Management deliverable known as "Expertise Locator" – a database of people and their specific skill sets. The community would self-advertise and field questions from colleagues around the globe. Unfortunately, the desired collaboration was between U.S. and Japanese scientists, and there were cultural and scientific norms in place that frowned upon asking for help.

What Happened? This project never got beyond the concept phase. Culture and behavioral norms can have a powerful impact; it can be overcome, but not without patience and understanding.

Money as Motivator

In the early days of the hype around CRM, there were plenty of low- and high-end systems available. The team was looking for something in the middle in terms of cost and capabilities. The target user group was in the Medical Marketing area of a pharmaceutical company, and like most sales-oriented individuals, defined their value to the company by who and what they knew.

What would ever provide an incentive to them to capture that knowledge in a database for *anyone* to use? Well, the group's manager had the right idea. He made quarterly bonuses dependent upon the quantity and content of the data entered into the system.

What Happened? The implementation was quite successful. Never underestimate the motivation of coin-operated individuals.

You Were Serious About That?

A small sales team in a B2B situation with multiple locations wanted to target a simple low-end CRM platform to manage their customer relationships. They were ready to roll something out for the entire global team – 30 users with 24x7 access and full database synchronization. The internal analyst knew the team well – salt of the earth, relationship sellers, etc. – and did not really want to invest in infrastructure unless they were serious. So, she set up a trial run, with three of the team members fully installed, syncing and sharing their data. After a few weeks, they realized that the only way to get value out of the database was to make sure they entered all of their conversations and connections.

What Happened? Most people want to read the information, but they do not want the task of typing it into the systems. Without data entry, the initiative was over. The project ended quietly before the team burned a lot of time and money configuring servers.

Elegant Digital Concepts May Be Overkill

An ambitious order-configurator project nearly ground to a halt from the lure of the "elegant user interface". The project sought to automate the layout of a complicated elevator fixture, with buttons, keys, and controls that were subject to extremely complicated ADA rules for accessibility, UL rules for safety, local building codes, and the physical limitations of the components. A difficult task was made worse as the project sponsor insisted on the "user-friendly" drag-and-drop ideas behind popular commercial packages.

What Happened? Unfortunately, the folks who understood all the configuration rules did not have a clue how to translate their knowledge into the object-oriented constructs required. A lot of detail and time was lost in the translation.

Heads in the Sand

A custom truck-trailer components manufacturer was often frustrated by his engineering group, who kept saying things could not be designed and delivered to meet specifications. Unfortunately, smaller local competitors kept figuring out how to do the impossible. The CEO often acquired local expertise to solve the problem, rather than figure it out within the four walls of his R&D group.

> **What Happened?** *Resistance to thinking in new ways* put many opportunities to bring value to the customer in danger. This inflexibility created hard times for the business, and heartburn for the CEO.

An excellent way to engage your teams is to get them to tell their own stories from the past. Ask for particularly good experiences, and particularly horrible experiences. I'm serious – ask the question specifically in that way, and just sit back and listen to how people react. Their responses will tell you a lot about their acceptance of change and how they approach the topic. Heck, it's a great interview question for new hires as you grow. I like to ask the question and then listen; a lot of what I am looking for is in the way they answer the question. And be sure to give people credit if they walked away from their experiences with some lessons learned.

Facilitating Innovation: An Environment of Possibilities

In some organizations, the strategic imperative driving a Digital Transformation is the need for "innovation." This buzzword can be tough to define, and even tougher to initiate. Teams typically see success where there is also a core understanding about the nature of innovation. It is not necessarily something you can prescriptively make happen. $X + Y = Innovation!$ A more likely, more natural approach is to establish an environment of possibilities by bringing together the ingredients – people, skills, imagination, time, and most important of all, freedom to experiment and freedom to fail.

Think of this as an *Environment of Possibilities* – a fascinating stew, a mixture of energy and raw materials, where ideas smash into each other, mixing and separating and reforming into things you were not really expecting. The theory, of course, is that good things will emerge out of this melting pot; meaningful ideas that create value and deliver results.

But getting something like this started in most organizations can be a challenge. It is a different way of thinking, and change rarely comes easily. What are some of the interesting questions that arise about the nature of innovation and the ingredients for an "environment of possibilities"?

The Current Environment

Rapid innovation comes about when the environment allows it and the skill sets enable it. An "environment of possibility" just means that folks are given time to experiment with digital concepts and ideas, and have access to the resources required to play around a bit. The challenge, of course, is providing time, training classes, and other resources to experiment. Effective leaders should invest in their teams; it does not take much to build a test environment and have folks start teaching themselves, making mistakes, and learning what works!

Innovation skills reside in everyone. But just like any other activity, success is 10 percent inspiration and 90 percent perspiration. Individuals, teams, and organizations need to build their innovation muscles by *doing*. A critical requirement here is that the organization must communicate that it is okay to fail. The corporate culture must expect a certain failure rate for new ideas. History should expose which tactics to avoid, but not necessarily which strategies will fail. Opportunity will be a mix of many things, and what was true at one time may no longer be true now.

The "How-To" Questions

How does leadership successfully position a think tank or innovation team so that it is (a) buffered from mundane corporate operations and politics, while (b) it remains sufficiently connected to executive leadership and operating divisions for its ideas to be acted upon? (I'm assuming that this "skunk works" is outside the normal corporate business structure.)

This is an incredibly important question. Skills and environment aside, successful innovation only happens when the team is sufficiently empowered to get ideas implemented. Sometimes this comes from executive sponsorship, but not as often as one might think! The cynical or faint of heart prefer to wait until they are granted permission to work on a project or idea.

People in your organization succeed because they have vision, drive, energy, and knowledge of how things work in a company. They know the lay of the land and use this knowledge to their advantage. Sometimes, these are long-time employees who have established relationships with those who control key people, resources, and decisions. At other times, these may be uber-techies who already know how the various pieces of process and technology work. This helps them identify resistors who throw obstacles in the way; citing budgets, approvals, policies, and difficult systems as reasons to halt progress. Note that you do not have to be a long-term member of the organization to be successful; new employees, with experiences from multiple industries, organization, technologies, etc. can be successful if they have the imagination and drive.

Leaders need to stack the deck for their innovation teams, by making a few simple, but powerful moves.

Carve out time in the schedule: Don't just add this to the long list of ToDos on everyone's plate. Take something off!

Provide visible executive sponsorship: You need to be able to pull that card out occasionally, to keep things moving.

Staff the team with a mix: You need the right blend of long-term and newer employees.

Identify a team leader: Target someone with the right mix of hands-on technical, business, and relationship-building skills. This cannot be an administrative role only. An effective team leader must be able to add expertise to the project, spot opportunity through the hype, understand how it translates to business value, and then communicate that effectively and concisely to those who need to support it.

Hold their feet to the fire: The team should have goals and objectives; this is not a license to play!

Let them fail: The most successful baseball players fail 70 percent of the time! Also, your skunk works team must remain connected to operations. The team will have to implement the big ideas eventually, and it is always good to remain grounded in reality. Make participation on the team part time for most; consider rotating different people in from various areas of the company so that everyone has a chance, and all remain connected to the base business.

What lessons have you learned from the skunk works experience that you can apply to the innovation process? What broad, meta issues and narrower specific issues has your project illuminated and solved (or at least, what questions has it posed)?

Aside from the organizational and change issues mentioned previously, you will find that innovation efforts often target things that are perceived as issues, but are actually symptoms of more fundamental behavioral or structural problems.

For example, collaboration tools and techniques are often lauded as new ways to unlock the wisdom of crowds, connect with the new generation in the workforce, or counter the flight of knowledge leaving the company upon retirement. Unfortunately, some of these efforts struggle, because what works on the Internet (with millions of users) does not always work at a corporation (with hundreds)[16].

Also, it always seems to boil down to Change Management – an overused buzz phrase that just says change is difficult. There are many ways to address this (education, repetition, participation), but management always needs to understand that corporate operating processes typically do not catch on like consumer products – here today, gone tomorrow.

The Spark to Ignite Your Innovation Ideas

As time marches on, and conversations around innovation, disruption, and Digital Transformation are maturing in many organizations, you can start to sense frustration. Some industries are changing in dynamic and exciting ways, with interesting new technology, energetic and engaged teams, and customers and markets that are accepting, even demanding, change. At least, those are the stories that make the headlines – the 20 percent of the world that is seeing 80 percent of the impact. How about that long tail of organizations, teams, and markets that cannot seem to break through and get the participation, the support, or the interest? What about the rest of us?

These are great topics to investigate over the conference table or a stack of bacon waffles. There are many unique and nuanced reasons for the frustration; every situation is unique, no matter how hard we try to establish patterns, put things in buckets, and focus on the critical few.

---

[16] (MacLennan 2006)

What's Missing?

Many organizations prefer action, and see the challenges inherent in moving forward with projects to make change happen. People are comfortable talking about *What* work needs to be done, and *How* the work should move forward.

Progress inevitably slows, and focus boils down to a short list of topics.

Resources: More than just budget, this includes time, attention, and great technology to do something different. We either can't get what we need at all, or we can't get enough, no matter what tradeoffs we make.

Opportunity: Does the organization want this? Does the market want this? Even if we can get a few nibbles of interest, we cannot close the deal, or get the whole organization to make the shift in focus.

Permission: This product idea seems to make sense, but there are stakeholders or gatekeepers in the way. Or can we manufacture permission by keeping things off the radar screen?

But it's still not enough ... what's missing?

The Hardest Part?

Often, the missing ingredient that leads to frustration is the *Why*.

> *Why are you talking about this?*

> *Why does the customer care?*

> *Why should we change?*

If your Digital Transformation process is not thoughtful about defining the *Why*, all of your efforts could look like an exercise in creativity. If you want to introduce change – to a team, an organization, a customer, a market – there must be a compelling reason.

> *What are we trying to accomplish?*

> *What has changed?*

> *Why do I care?*

> *What's in it for me?*

How does this align to our mission and vision?

Why should we make this pivot, change course, or add this to our current objectives?

For those headline-grabbing stories that create 80 percent of the impact – the *Why* was (and is) tremendously obvious, forced upon them, and/or driven by a force with vision and resources.

We must all focus on our own compelling *Why*, and help our teams, markets, and people see why they care about resources and opportunities. And most of all – we need to help them understand they have the *permission* and are empowered to make change.

A compelling *Why* can be the spark to light your initiative on fire. Let's work on our understanding, and craft a meaningful message and vision to help others feel the energy.

Field Notes: Getting to Why

One conversation in particular helped me crystallize an approach that focuses on the importance of what motivates change. A friend and I were discussing their innovation approach in a typical conservative midwestern manufacturing company.

"Okay," said my technically astute friend, "I understand all of that 'focus on the why' stuff – but I still have many questions, and many frustrations, since I can't seem to get the attention of the decision makers. Technology innovations are coming fast and thick: robot bartenders, brilliant slot cars, fitness trackers, and chasing Pokémon around town ..."

"Seriously? You went in with 'Pokémon'?"

"No no no... I mean, yes... but look what those things represent –advanced automation, artificial intelligence, IoT and analytics, or augmented reality. How can we get Marketing or Product Development to understand and appreciate how this cool new technology can bring innovation to our company?"

"Well, there's your first mistake," I countered, "because your question is flawed from the outset. You are so focused on the *How* – the technology – but you completely skipped over the *Why*."

This is a classic mistake that technologists routinely make – focusing on technology for technology's sake.

"Fine," my friend continued, "then how do we make that next step? How do we get to the right *Why*?"

"Just ask the key stakeholders who are making the decisions," I explained. "Does your organization drive priorities from what the shareholders on Wall Street are expecting? What about the Board, or Executive Management? Are important initiatives handed down from above? Or consider the local General Manager or the Functional Area leads. What is listed in their Goal Deployment plans, or annual Performance Objectives?"

"Seriously? That approach doesn't sound very original or innovative."

"Exactly," I said, "because we aren't trying to innovate the act of introducing change! Try to flip your point of view, and approach it from the other direction. Ask the people on the front lines who interact directly with your customers. Or ask your customers themselves. What are they looking for? What important needs are they finding hard to fill? What's missing?"

"Sounds simple," said my friend, "but how exactly are we supposed to get input from the customer or front-line employees? They aren't publishing their requirements on the intranet, or in those long and detailed slide decks that we get from management."

I smiled on the inside – a classic question, one that I have asked myself over the years, countless times.

"Just ask them! Go out on the floor, among the cubicles, out to the sales meetings. Ask to ride along on service calls, or join in on the customer visits. Just talk to them. They'll probably be happy someone is actually listening, and loaded with practical, valuable ideas on applying innovative thinking, tools, and processes."

"And here's the trick," I continued. "You have to hold these opinions, this input, at an equal level of value with the direction you are getting from above. Management will tell you what the big initiatives are, but your front-line folks are the ones having the daily conversations with paying customers."

These two groups – *front line* and *customers* – are the most important constituents in this value-generating, innovation-hungry system. Listen to what they are saying, and then make that message fit with the big picture ideas from the corporate powers-that-be.

Better yet – ignore the buzzwords, pay attention to the real, meaningful needs that are being expressed, and make "bottom up" input the real *Why* of your innovation ideas.

The *customer* is the one
   who makes the ultimate purchase decision.

The *front line* team members are the ones
   who deliver on the promise.

Everything else is just chasing the latest shiny thing.

Chapter 10

How Can My Team Participate?

The success of your Digital Business will be driven by your teams' ability to come together in a new and different way. Diverse areas of expertise need to mix and merge, bringing their unique strengths to the table to create something that is bigger than the sum of its parts.

The attraction of a Digital Transformation is the exciting future of technology that promises to change the *action* parts of our jobs (how we do what we do), as well as the *thinking* parts (how we get better at it). The challenge of a Digital Transformation is the entrenched power of the "as-is" – the current state that has stubbornly clung to how your organization thinks and acts, every day. Helping your organization make that change is always the toughest part. To increase the odds of success, everyone on your team needs to leverage the power of the current state – the skills and capabilities developed over the years – to enable, and really drive to the exciting future and ensure its success.

Each functional area needs to understand the skills and strengths that they bring to the effort; why do they deserve a "seat at the table"? Your organization will not be magically gifted with a well-written playbook of detailed instructions on how to make this transformation happen. The change must come from within.

So how can you, in your specific functional area, bring transformational change to the organization? Let's walk through the org chart and capture some thoughts.

Sales and Marketing

Perhaps the most visible and exciting part of your Digital Transformation is the chance to bring "cool stuff" from the world of consumer technology into the realm of business-to-business commerce. There are many lessons that old-line B2B companies take from this hyper-competitive, consumer-focused world of B2C, and expectations are growing for B2B companies to present themselves more like the consumer companies that we deal with in our daily personal lives.

> *Why is it that my electronic life at home is so much better than my electronic life at work? Why do the screens have to look this way? Why does it have to be so hard to get information? Why can't I "google" and "app" my way through the business day?*

The Marketing team is often best positioned to truly understand what is happening in the world of consumer electronics and consumer digital capabilities – the Darwinian impact of rapid and continuous iteration with highly engaged customers in a highly competitive market. This style of development and change has driven a focus on *design* – for eye appeal, but more importantly, for easy-to-understand process, elegantly designed flow, and an extreme focus on understanding where value is created.

In this environment, what can Marketing bring to the table to drive your Digital Transformation?

Design Thinking for Process

So many legacy internal systems and processes are blessed with legendary difficulty. People love to complain about how tough it is to enter customer data, transact orders, or ship products. And let's not limit our thinking to technology; how many of us still rail against the amazing bureaucracy that springs up out of nowhere in organizations? This is truly a case where size does not matter. Even the smallest companies can create strangely archaic processes that are insensitive to the user.

The Marketing team must explain your products and services in a way that customers can easily understand; Sales often must get involved to help customers navigate your customer service function so we can get the invoice to them and get their payment quickly. The same ideas and experiences are applicable to your internal process. There is a great opportunity for customer-sensitive folks to apply simplification and clear communications to make your internal teams' daily work more effective.

Design Thinking for Information

How about applying design thinking to the complex information that comes out of our systems? We have all labored through illegible spreadsheets printed in the tiniest font because someone insisted that these reports should all fit on a single sheet of paper. And how many times can we watch another presentation loaded with bullet points and poorly justified text showing badly presented ideas that could easily be summarized into a single picture or a three-point set of priorities? Visualizing the insights that are trapped in data sets can be a difficult task. Communicating the complexity of ideas is an area where Marketing absolutely can lead the team.

Voice of the Customer

Successful Marketing teams are already tuned in and listening to the customer, understanding their requirements, and designing solutions to service those needs. So why is it hard to apply that same kind of thinking to internal processes? Why can't we think of our peers in the organization – the other functional areas that must interact with these processes, understand the customer information, or work with products? Why don't we think of those folks as customers? And if we see them as customers, shouldn't we be listening to their thoughts and ideas on how to improve these processes? When we pivot our thinking like this, we will more effectively listen to and understand them, and this new way of working will have a big impact. You do not have to be a paying customer to be treated like a person.

Identifying Value

At the start of the day, Sales and Marketing helps external customers understand our products and the value that they bring. This is a process of education and effective communication; we are introducing new capabilities, trying to get our customers to change their minds and processes, and invest their time and money differently. This is a difficult task, but powerful when done well.

We can apply the same thinking to the change required when going through a Digital Transformation. This is a process of education and effective communication in which we are introducing new ways of thinking and new ways of leveraging digital techniques to change the way we operate, connect, and provide value. This ability to communicate the idea of value, and understand how to make it personal for the folks who need to make the change, is a critical skill that Sales and Marketing can bring to bear and coach their peers on building these skills.

Profitable Revenue

At the end of the day, Sales and Marketing must ensure that our products and services generate more revenue than the cost required to manufacture and distribute them. Every new dollar is not as good as the last; most companies operate on the idea that steady earnings growth and solid, predictable cash flow are large components of the Enterprise Value equation. This is where Sales and Marketing can make a difference – by understanding what it takes to set the price of a product such that a sustainable business can be built around it. In the same way, the organization has to understand the maximum amount of value that these transformational Digital ideas will bring to the company, and what the offsetting cost (in time, effort, and angst) will be required.

Transformation is change; and Sales and Marketing are arguably the teams with the most experience in introducing change successfully. Organizations are used to transforming for external customers. Now you must turn your attention to your internal teammates.

Product Management

When your Digital Business is looking toward the products component and adding information as a new and differentiating feature, there will be initial resistance across the board. Information-enabled products can represent a big departure from the norm, and can be confusing, even jarring, on the organizations' world view. The Product Management team can drive this part of your Digital Business by applying traditional skills and insights to these new and different types of products, especially when your team is having limited success after floating a few ideas past the decision makers.

This is not an aberration; there are plenty of companies experiencing the same roadblocks during these early years of digital products. We can't all work in firms that sell in high volume to consumers who are actively looking for the next smart gadget. Industrial IoT is loaded with great ideas, but challenged with markets, channels, and customer segments that are conservative and slow to change.

Or so people say... but there *are* success stories floating around that are validating our suspicions about the appetite for these kinds of products. The world is seeing more industries, markets, and niche-y applications that are aggressively and successfully pulling information and technology into their success formulas. Obviously, some product teams are figuring out the critical recipe for getting approval, making the investment, and bringing these solutions to market.

Success patterns are emerging; one has to do with breaking through that initial resistance to change. To get an idea off the ground, there are four important ingredients that can make the transformation happen. Not all of these are required, but you must have *at least* two of these to have any chance of getting things moving.

- **A Smart Idea**: Many folks think that a unique, innovative smart idea is all that is required to launch a successful product. After all, they have depth of experience in their markets and technical domains. Add in some exposure and/or experience with sensors and data analytics, and a little imagination when it comes to the power of artificial intelligence – why wouldn't the market just fall in love with this idea? Many will review (again) the amazing tale of Steve Jobs and the iPhone, and mention other cherry-picked stories of disruptive technologies. But those stories are about unicorns – relatively rare events. In the industrial world, conservative niche markets and customers can be amazingly resistant to these ideas.

Nope, this is not enough. We are going to have to add *at least* one of the following:

- **Customer Pull**: Successful companies know that listening to your customers and understanding their wants and needs is table stakes for growth. When you get specific requirements (or requests) for operational and performance data that is tied to your products, you have found an ally in your drive for change. Smart leaders looking for growth cannot resist a paying customer standing at the door with dollars in their hand, ready to buy, if we can just deliver on their requirements.

- **Competitive Threat**: If you really understand the forces at play in your markets, and you are building a proper product strategy, you will learn about competitive threats. When your competition is making the move to smart, connected products before you are – and threatening to take market share – it is easier to define the imperative, and develop at least an equivalent offering.

- **Leadership Buy-In**: Of course, if you have a general manager, managing director, president, or product line leader with the vision and the will to make a change, it will happen. Resistance to new and different ideas will come from inside and outside of your organization, and a visionary leader can help educate and advocate.

Again, you must have *at least two* of these four ingredients if you really want this product idea to take off. If you have only one, what do you do? And how can your product management experience help bridge the gap?

Get Alignment

If you are missing that critical buy-in from your leadership, you need to spend some quality time with them to understand where the gap is. Start by listening.

What are the critical objectives for your organization? If the focus is on cost containment, talent development, M&A – basically, everything *except* new product development – then why are you surprised? You must get aligned with the critical few priorities to get their attention and support.

Get Understanding

The decision makers in your organization may have a bias against significant change in the core technology of your products. Going from the physical world of products to the virtual world of services is a wildly different engineering and operations paradigm. I call it "widgets to digits," and it represents a fundamentally different way of thinking, operating, and staffing. The technology may sound fun and look cool, but the reality can be daunting.

How can you overcome this challenge? Start with clear product development and operations plans, fully loaded with the costs and the timing. Build a complete business case that outlines the expected revenue and share gain, and hold that up against these costs. And tie it to the things your leadership values; if your ideas do not line up with the priorities of the decision makers, they will have no time or interest.

Get Informed

A great way to get the organization's attention and shift priorities to new products is to get that "pull" from customers, or that "push" from competition. Do not try to bank on your smart idea, cooked up on a lab bench in the back room, to be enough. Get out in the field and connect with real customers, and get them involved in the design.

If you think you have the germ of a smart idea, build a minimum viable product[17] to help people understand the direction of your vision. That is all you need to get out and talk with your customers. They are real people immersed in tough challenges – the problems that you would like to solve for them. Your customers can describe the problems and make them real; they will tell you what is right and wrong about your solution in very pointed and valuable ways. In fact, they will probably tell you how to either simplify your approach, or redirect your energies and do something that they *will* pay for.

Do not forget to research your competition as well, searching for inbound threats. If you do not know what the other side is doing, you are destined to get blind-sided. It's not that tough; go to a trade show and walk the aisles. Talk to your customers and ask them why they are not buying your solution over the competitor's. Typically, industrial markets are fairly open with information like this, and it is relatively easy to get a pulse on what's happening.

Get Experimenting

It's tough to manufacturer a smart idea out of nothing. A little curiosity and energy help, and there are plenty of entry-level tech components and tutorials to develop your understanding of what

---

[17] Minimum Viable Product, or MVP, is a concept taken from the work of Eric Ries. It is entirely reasonable, and quite effective, to take ideas from the digital startup world, and apply them to more traditional corporate product development efforts. (Ries 2011)

is possible. If you understand the basics of how things work, you can apply these ideas to your marketplace, your customers, and your problem domain.

Remember, information and technology are changing the nature of your products, and they represent a very real risk. How can you eliminate the risk and gain approval?

Product Development

When introducing the idea of "information as a product or service," it is fascinating to see how different teams want to start. I do not mean *start the conversation* – that part of the process seems to take care of itself. Hallway conversations and chats over a beer can gauge initial interest; when the team sits down for your first chalk talk, the IoT Building Blocks[18] help to keep things going.

Where does a business unit, a product line, or an engineering team *start the journey*? Remember, industrial manufacturers historically (and quite correctly) see their role as "making and shipping products," and the shift to "providing and supporting data-enabled products" is a pretty big leap. New ideas rarely occur in a vacuum; there are plenty of other development efforts underway. Few teams have spare time on their hands, looking for a Next Big Project to fill the idle hours.

Over the past few years, we have seen patterns emerge in how Product Development teams are adding information as a fundamental part of their offering. Let's look at five fictitious product lines in real categories.

Explorers: These teams come to the table with a specific destination in mind – a new product or product extension, maybe some data analysis for customers or internal engineering – but they are not quite sure how to get there. Typically, they are taking an evolutionary step from a product or capability that they already have. MobileCo, for example, manufactures add-ons for trucks, transports and tractors, and has access to all the operating data

---

[18] from Chapter 6

in real time. Their big idea is to capture that data and present it back to the end customer for predictive maintenance, billing automation, route optimization, and similar things.

How can you help them take the next step? Engage the team, find out who has energy, and start to sketch out a path to the end. You may find the end vision changing a bit as the team tries different routes, but most likely you will land upon one of the IoT Building Block components as the current roadblock. Spin up a mini project to attack that roadblock, and try to knock it down to get product development underway in earnest.

Spelunkers: These folks have a specific feature or capability in mind, but don't quite know how to translate that into something the customer will value. This could be a team that has not yet added sensors to the device, and are thinking too much on that piece of the framework. If there is no clear idea yet how end customers might make use of this data, then they are searching a dark cave for a spot of gold. DeviceCo is talking about pulling data from their awesome widgets, but they do not have a use case that is quickly and easily defined.

How can you help take the next step? Focus on the revenue potential; roughly speaking, how much income might an offering like this bring in annually? If the number is big enough, it might focus attention on the project. If you cannot figure out who would actually pay for such a feature, maybe it's best to ask customers where their interests lie.

Old Guard: Some groups already have software and systems as part of their product offering, and see IoT concepts as just another technology advancement. They are not resisting ideas from the outside, but they may be unaware how different (and difficult!) the tech challenges around mobile or cloud will be, or how their relationships with their customers and channels will change. GreybeardCo is a bit like this. They are well down their own path and are actively getting feedback from customers. They liked the breakdown of the Building Blocks and are interested in hearing more as bits of that get fleshed out.

How can you help take the next step? Share whatever good information you have – project templates, business plans, technology components, and stories of success and failure – and invite these folks to do the same with their intellectual property. The "old guard" can benefit by bringing in new thinking and new possibilities. The rest of the digital community can benefit by sharing technology and knowledge that has brought value to the old guard.

Watchers: For some, this entire conversation is brand new and totally unexpected. *"Why are we talking about this?"* Of course, when the lead-in is all about increasing revenues and share price with innovative technology, they do listen, and may even lean into the brainstorming. But this was not likely on their radar screen when they completed their strategic plans for the coming year. With many competing priorities, this project may end up on the back burner. PatientCo fits into this "watch and wait" category. A recurring theme for well-run teams is to keep focused on a critical few tasks; this "IoT stuff" is a distraction from their well-laid plans.

How can you help take the next step? Provide visibility to and connection with other business lines and projects, and answer any questions these folks might have. Assure them that the Internet of Things is not something that they have to do via some corporate edict or fad-of-the-quarter. At the same time, suggest that they keep their ears to the ground. These topics may come up when talking with customers and channel partners, and they (and you) should be ready to pick up the conversation again.

Enthusiasts: There will always be the high energy folks who are asking you for help on IoT before you get a chance to ask first. They see the opportunity, and may even see forces inside their own markets signaling intent and making moves already. They have the vision, but no path to get there – no sensors on devices, no experience in the tech, and a few preliminary ideas on how to monetize it. HackerCo fits into this category – a company with a combination of insightful product line management and a market space that is being aggressively pushed into the information age by major OEMs.

How can you help take the next step? Latch on and support as much as possible, and drive the conversation to something specific and actionable. It might be a mini-project, a little proof-of-concept, that gets management or customers thinking big; or, it could be some structured thinking and dialogue to focus on a single target, a first deliverable that will get the ball rolling. At the same time, start educating the team about the need for an overall process and technology architecture that you will need to build toward in anticipation of explosive growth.

Operations

The everyday internal operations of your company should be the most mature area for applied digital technology. Experience is a great teacher, and internal processes in the enterprise have been subjected to evolutionary changes for many years. This should give the Operations team a significant advantage in understanding the potential for digital techniques, as well as the non-digital work required to make the technology-enabled elements scalable and sustainable.

There is truth and wisdom in our collected experience, and we can learn a lot from non-digital internal processes. I like to point out that "When you automate a mess, you get an automated mess." It is an old truism from my digital youth, and still holds true today. Operations teams have developed skills and techniques in understanding how to streamline the business by taking cost and effort out of their daily work. So Operations is in a key position to leverage this experience, and show leadership in your Digital Transformation in a number of important ways.

Eliminate Waste

The specific types of waste targeted by the principles of Lean Manufacturing are all applicable in digital conversations. Operations can leverage their skills in Lean to identify and eliminate waste (overproduction, wait time, transportation, extra processing, unnecessary inventory, excess motion, defects) in all aspects of the business, including how you connect with customers, handle and process data, and interact and collaborate among teams.

Eliminate Complexity

Similarly, your Operations team should be the most skilled at applying the Pareto principle, understanding that 80 percent of the value is realized by 20 percent of your effort (tasks, projects, time). This 80/20 rule can be applied in many ways, and when Operations uses it to eliminate complexity introduced by the 80 percent of processes that generate only 20 percent of the results, the impact can be amazing.

Eliminating waste and reducing complexity will free up a lot of important resources, not the least of which are time and attention. Your Digital Transformation efforts will be much more impactful with focus; the Operations team will have the biggest impact when they help your organization focus on the critical few things that are required. But do not stop there – Operations can provide leadership in other areas as well:

Team Communication

Another standout tactic of Lean Manufacturing practitioners is the idea of a Daily Stand-Up meeting. As the day begins, cross-functional teams get together to review the hot items of the day, follow up on yesterday's priorities, and make sure the collective focus is on critical customers and shipments for the day. No technology has to be involved; the focus is on simple charts and open conversation among the teams. This practice is a great example of direct collaboration at the point of impact.

Management by Metrics

Effective Operations teams have learned to use metrics (specifics, data, facts) to understand what is happening around them and focus their attention where it needs to be focused. Again, this is an area in which many have experienced success with minimal technology. It's not about how you process the data, it's how you use the information to change your behavior. Technology often comes into play as the metrics get more sophisticated and opportunities for improvement become more pointed. But the technology is secondary to the impact that we are trying to create.

Be the Beta User

Innovative R&D engineers are talking about information as a new and differentiating feature for the products we sell to our customers. But the idea of using sensors and smart devices to measure and monitor machines is not new. Operations has been experimenting with Machine-to-Machine (M2M) technology for years. So why not get these two groups together to try some of these information-enabled machine ideas internally? Your Operations team can act like a primary beta-user for these new products, and R&D can do some experimenting and valuable learning (i.e. failing) with the most understanding type of customer. Your learning events (mistakes) only impact internal operations, and keeps the interruptions away from external customers. It is also a great way for key folks on the product management team (especially engineers!) to get their own hands-on experience to demystify this magical technology and make it digestible for the conservative organization.

Field Notes: Hidden Gold in Automating Recurring Processes

There are many practical applications for applying digital thinking to your Operational systems and processes, and many opportunities for Operations to "volunteer" in this beta user role. Here is a typical scenario: each quarter, you need to audit user access to a critical application. Internal security standards require that you revoke access for those who have not been on the system for more than 90 days. I have seen this issue in many companies, and the difficulties are all too common.

- It's manual; the team did a quick-and-dirty set of steps years ago to cover the minimum requirements that involve extracts from application logs, file transfers and spreadsheets, and some emails.

- It's not drop-dead simple, because there is a list of exceptions – multiple user IDs that were always kept active, even if they have not been used.

- The overall process was never documented.

Coupled with the fact that this only happened once per quarter and involved less than five total effort hours to take care of, the easy response is to get the task done and move on. But this is penny wise and pound foolish; there are long-term quality problems to be avoided, and short-term opportunities for internal staff development that are being ignored.

Problem: If we continued to just do the minimum amount of work to satisfy the requirement, it was no surprise that over time, steps were omitted. The lack of documentation forced folks to repeat steps from memory, and pass along the process word-of-mouth as roles rotated and/or people turned over.

Opportunity: Simplifying things required some automation; nothing too difficult, but definitely interesting and non-trivial. For example, we needed a custom database for tracking project work. Simple enough, but extra effort was required to get supporting controls in place – time investments that we chose to skip in previous years. We finally bit the bullet, attacked the backlog of work, and built the tracking system. We solved the problem, and saw some unanticipated benefit; the project became a perfect training opportunity for staff members looking to build software development skills. This was a small system, so it was a small risk, small time requirement, and a perfect filler for those burnt out on big projects and in need of an escape.

Of course, the push-back was always the same: "*I have no time for this.*" Most can easily envision a total solution that is simple, uses familiar technology, gets rid of the multiple platforms and manual processes, and is sustainable. In this case, however, it would take about 16-32 effort hours to get done, and who has the time?

The solution was to attack the problem in baby steps, and make the overall process a little better each time. For issues like this, you do not need to solve all your problems now, and it is okay to leave the work unfinished until next time. However, the key is that you must commit to making a small improvement each time you touch the process.

For example, the first pass on the user access audit opportunity looked like this:

- The current task owners walked through the process with the developer, who took down scratchy notes on paper and in a simple text file.

- The spreadsheet that tracked people and counted days was located. The developer added some simple code to automate counts and formulas for computing days since last log in.

- The data was sorted to show users who had not signed in for 90 days, which were then manually matched against the list of exception user IDs.

This work was a one-time add of a few hours of effort – a small start, but a platform on which to build.

After a few months, it was time for the second pass:

- The scratchy notes were moved to a shared document, and multiple authors started to iterate.

- The exceptions list was added to the spreadsheet to simplify the last manual matching step.

- The results were returned to the next person in the process, who no longer need to edit out exceptions – a step removed!

This work was another one-time add of two to three hours, but we had already simplified the overall process, and we saw the total effort (including process improvements) starting to decline.

The third pass included:

- A small programming project to build an exception table in a database and automate the log extracts. This only required a few hours of effort.

- A final cut was made at the process documentation in the shared area, and it was now ready to be turned it over to the operational support teams.

Note that each time you iterate on something like this, you need to feel comfortable with the idea that these works in process – these interim deliverables – are clearly unfinished, even raggedy. It should not matter, because each time you touch it, it gets a little bit better. Plus, the priority was originally low enough that a totally manual effort was okay.

Incremental improvements on the primary goal (automated user audits) with tasty side benefits along the way (mini side projects to keep stretching your tech chops) equals a win-win for everyone.

Finance

Data is a core asset of a Digital Business, and Finance is the functional area that has been deeply involved with data and information for the longest time. Makers make, Shipping ships, Customer Service serves customers, Marketers educate, and Sellers sell – important roles that reflect the value as it is delivered to your customers. Finance has always been the profession of numbers, accounting for costs and revenues and tracking the value of the company and what we produce. This long pedigree of speaking in facts is reflected in the first wave of Digital impact – the automation of operations and the introduction of accounting systems and ERP.

Does this mean that Finance has a natural leadership role in your Digital Business? Probably not. Your business strategy talks about what you do, where you play, and how you win. Operational details like accounting for it all are just that – required, important, but not necessarily what differentiates the organization.

Does that mean that Finance has no seat at the table as you plan and execute your Digital Transformation? On the contrary. With their depth of experience with data and information, Finance can and should play a critical role. As you think through each of the Five Components, these simple yet powerful ideas can inspire your Finance teams to apply the critical strengths and capabilities, and bring those strengths and capabilities to the other functional teams.

Speaking in Facts

Core systems and processes that support the operations of the company – think Accounting, ERP, and other planning systems – have long been an important concentration area of the Finance team. A popular buzzword in this area is *metrics*, or KPIs; you cannot manage something if you can't measure it. This is a concept that works best when subtly and deftly applied.

Finance is often best positioned to understand the applicability of a metric, and the most logical way of gathering the data. Your Finance organization can make a huge impact by helping the other areas of your Digital Business speak in facts, at the right level of detail, to make impactful decisions.

Structure for Scale and Sustainability

Many new digital systems and processes have been introduced since the dawn of the Internet – ever more accessible technology that can quickly be deployed to impact our customers and our relationships with them. This has been a mixed blessing; in a relatively short period of time, we have seen multiple examples of hastily implemented and resourced systems that cannot scale with the growth of the business. Poorly implemented processes are fundamentally unsustainable, and far too reliant on key individuals or value chain partners to keep them from falling over.

With their depth of experience in operational systems, Finance should be able to ward off these outcomes by sharing techniques for managing complexity, managing master data, and creating processes that can be passed on to new teams and new people as needs change.

Identifying Value

The excitement of new technologies like sensors, data, and informatics applied to older, more traditional physical products is like a siren call to Engineering and Product Development teams searching for that breakthrough idea to spur sales and market share growth. All too often, the product teams have a difficult time understanding how to create value, and how to accurately plan for supporting and sustaining this value over time.

Finance is usually in the best position to understand how shareholder value is created for your company, and the levels of risk and investment that the organization will accept. Who better to help characterize a new product's value proposition? In addition, product teams that are comfortable making and selling widgets probably have little experience with digits and the costs involved in building and supporting these types of services. Finance needs to help product teams upgrade their business plan templates to account for new patterns of revenue ramps, new metrics to understand go/no-go points, and new costs structures to get where they need to be.

New Skills for Sustainable Teams

With the mass of data coming from all of these silos (Operations, Customers, Products), the task of pulling out information and insights that will drive your Digital Business forward becomes more complex. When you fully understand each step in the Data Value Chain[19], you realize that a breadth of skills is required, ranging from Insight and Design to Science and Execution. Combined with the ever-changing list of supporting technologies (including all the latest buzzwords, like Big Data, Machine Learning, and Cloud), the critical component here is decidedly non-technical. Finance can and should lead the way in developing teams with this broad range of skills to leverage the information, but to do it in a way that scales with growth and sustained value even when there is turnover on the team.

Partnering Means Collaboration:

It is something of a buzzword heard in Finance circles – the idea that we must be *partners* with the different functional areas of the business. Others might use the term *collaboration*, but the value of this approach and its challenges are similar. Most folks understand the value proposition behind the words, but true partnership and collaboration across organizational lines and even across geographies (time and space) require a different set of skills. Your Digital Business must learn to think and work differently, and Finance may be in the best position to teach by example, showing the rest of the company how it is done.

---

[19] from Chapter 7

The Digital Project Budget

When pitching a new digital project to management, you want a clear line of sight to the value you are going to create – hard $$ (new revenue, margin expansion, increased share), soft $$ (customer lock-in, better competitive position), and/or productivity. But too many teams fail to lay out the cost side of the equation very well. This typically leads to some common behavior patterns:

The Zero Investment Tactic: "These ideas are too new, and they'll never approve this, so I'm doing it as a side project on my own time. It's all based on open source, so all I need is a college intern looking for a semester project. My nephew knows something about computers, and he built a web page once...."

Conversations that start like this are amusing in the face of the grand amounts of value that people are confident will be generated. If we plan on making $2 million in year one, why not spend $500,000 to get it built quickly and with some hope of scalability?

The One Number I Know: If custom or packaged software is required, or if SaaS (online) is the answer, managers will get a price quote from the vendor or an estimate from the developer, and get budget approval for that number and no more. A budget like that has no chance of success, as there is no time or investment planned for hardware, hosting, implementation services, or integration to other systems. And most digital solutions will need ongoing care and feeding, training and tuning, and multiple supporting processes. Is the existing team going to give up some of their current work, or are we adding incremental headcount?

The Integration and Data Quality Assumptions: It is extremely rare that the problem we are looking at through the digital lens is new and "unattached." Typically, the team is interested in automating transactions, providing access to information for customers, or discovering trends and opportunities with some witty analytics. "The information is right there in my ERP, website, product catalog, CRM system, click streams, HR/Payroll database, CAD drawings. If I can just present it better, or make it available on my mobile phone...."

The truth is, the big chunk of work will come in the areas of data quality (...this new and unanticipated use of our data is changing our requirements) and/or integration (...how am I going to get data in and out of the new system). Few systems or services come fully integrated with every data source in your unique world.

There are many ways to address these patterns, but let's not throw a wet blanket on these great ideas. Diving immediately into the cost and planning details will be counterproductive and will slow your progress, especially at the beginning of the project when you are trying to seize an opportunity, and generate excitement and support. At this stage, you just need a simple cost structure to accompany the benefits definition of the project. You understand how much it is worth, but you need to understand how much it is going to cost.

The cost elements of any digital project[20] are going to lay out like this **Digital Project Budget**:

People / Talent		One Time	Recurring
Staff	New skills to build / maintain	120,000	
Staff	Add-on for supporting processes		80,000
Travel & Training			15,000
Outside Labor	Contractors, Temps	50,000	10,000
Technology / Assets			
Hardware	Lease / Buy + Maintenance	30,000	
Software	Buy + Maintenance	15,000	
Telecomm / Data			10,000
Technology / Services			
Infrastructure	Cloud-based compute and storage	25,000	100,000
Platforms	Cloud-based environments	5,000	10,000
Other			
Depreciation			15,000
	Total	245,000	240,000

Digital Project Budget

There are a few major benefits here:

- **Simple + Complete Cost Picture**: For the executive approver, nothing says *I know what I am talking about and I've thought*

---

[20] (MacLennan, The Digital Project Budget: How Much? 2014)

this through like a comprehensive cost structure that is quick and easy to understand.

- **Risk Reduction**: Covering all of the cost elements will force you to think of the big picture, and not just the sale price from the vendor rep who is trying to make his quarterly numbers. Reducing risk of the unknown is another plus for our executive sponsor.
- **Comparing Alternatives**: It should be just as simple to build a complete cost model for competing alternatives. This is a great way to show that this option has the best cost profile (once you have established that doing nothing is not viable).

This structure also addresses two of the bad behavior patterns above:

- **The One Number I Know**: If you fill in the grid completely, you will have a lot more than just acquisition cost defined. Of particular value is the People/Talent section. You could replace the $$ with "work hours" or FTEs, but you have to call out that this will require incremental work.
- **The Integration and Data Quality Assumptions**: The Professional Services section should include a healthy amount of investment, unless you happen to have folks with human-centered design, big data, and integration development skills already on staff and with some free time on their hands.

Information Technology

There is an interesting phenomenon at companies looking at new and different ways to incorporate digital concepts into their businesses. There is a certain leap of faith (or hope) that the new and different steps in this journey will be easy. This is an extrapolation of our experience with internet search (thousands of answers from a simple question) and apps on smartphones (one click installation, connected to everything, and so easy to use). But when things get a teeny bit complicated, the local IT department is usually called.

Do not assume that IT has an obvious, critical, strategic position of power here. Most of the time, IT is called in to fill the gaps when the "simple instructions" that come in the box reach their limit. These are not conversations about architecture, process, or governance; this is "calling in the local techie to fix my problem."

How does your IT team break out of these support tasks and become an equal contributor? An important way to get the attention of the rest of the team is to focus on your critical strengths in each of the Five Components to understand the biggest impact that you bring to the table. Just as with the other functional areas, there are simple, powerful ideas that will focus your team.

Communicating Complexity

In most businesses, the IT department is the best source for project managers, especially for complex initiatives that impact multiple areas of the enterprise and require precision and coordination for technology-enabled processes. Most companies can identify with the big ERP implementations or upgrades – multi-headed projects managed with the classic waterfall method. These imposing efforts involve internally focused functions like Operations and Finance – departments that must commit time for a lot of one-time effort that they may not fully understand. At the other project management extreme, diverse teams in Marketing, Creative, and Analytics use an Agile approach with a focus on keeping the chunks of work small while iterating repeatedly to make sure the changes will fit the needs.

Call it what you will, but in the end, all project management methodologies tie to the same primary objective – managing expectations and communicating across a complex web of stakeholders and participants. This is where IT can make a huge difference – by leveraging your experience in managing complexity, and communicating with the affected teams effectively as your new digital ideas start to make their way through the established norms.

Help Me Listen

Communication is a bi-directional activity, and Digital Thinking can help us listen more effectively. When introducing new digital ideas for product features, customer connections, and internal processes, it can be surprisingly difficult for people to get meaningful feedback. IT is in a unique position to help in ways that satisfy your need for staying relevant and up to date with new technologies. Simply put, IT can help build prototypes and proof-of-concept experiments to quickly illustrate the possible, and help to make it real for folks considering something new.

The key here is speed – failing fast, iterating for impact, and pivoting to value where necessary. IT benefits from hands-on experience with shiny new tech, while Product teams can show prototypes and get precious Voice of the Customer feedback that tells you if you are going in the right direction.

Start Simple, Evolve to Sustainable

Prototypes and experiments bring a lot of impact in the early stages of a digital change event. IT must be comfortable with an important new requirement – the need to iterate quickly, and build objects that are not necessarily production-ready to get things moving. Keep it simple in the beginning, so the team can quickly identify the most impactful way to apply their new ideas.

Of course, there comes a time when simple and fast must transition to structured, scalable, and controlled. This transition often feels like things are slowing down, and it will frustrate the creative and energized new-tech thinkers in the organization. This is where IT must step up to manage that transition. It is important not to jump too early and stifle innovation; but do not wait until it is too late or things will spin out of control and value will be destroyed in waste and rework.

Run to the Magic

For some, the most exciting parts of digital are the new technology buzzwords that come our way – things like Cloud, AI, Big Data,

Machine Learning, Blockchain, and the Internet of Things. There is a big difference, however, between using a buzzword to sell an exciting idea, and understanding the buzzword enough to identify and demonstrate the actual value that can be created.

Arthur C. Clarke once wrote that, "Any sufficiently advanced technology is indistinguishable from magic."[21] That is a great way to describe the amazing opportunity for the technology-inclined in IT. The "magic" behind these buzzwords can be intimidating to decision-makers, but when your IT team can explain them in simple terms, and create early-stage prototypes that are relevant to your business, it can significantly accelerate things in the right direction.

IT must take time for some basic training and a more detailed look at this stuff. You will find that, for the most part, it is all a reasonable evolution from the familiar tech we already know. No, you will not become a qualified Data Scientist over a few weekends – if it was that easy, anyone could do it. But with a little extra effort, you can understand enough about this new technology to be able to drive the conversation and make it real.

Collaboration is Hard, So Show Them How

Finance likes to talk about *partnering*. IT teams like to talk about *collaboration*. To be fair, the concept is the same, but the tools and techniques are slightly different. Learning to work in an electronically collaborative environment is a difficult thing to do, and savvy IT teams will see the opportunity to lead the way by action, not words.

Collaboration and communication are difficult bi-directional processes. You must be a good learner, self-directed with a certain amount of curiosity to go out and find information. At the same time, your teams must hone their skills in capturing ideas in ways that other people can actually understand and use.

---

[21] (Clarke 1973)

We know what "good" looks like in this area – IT is very comfortable googling[22] for their everyday answers. Your IT team must learn from that experience and turn it inward, driving the use of collaboration tools and processes to really understand how to make it work in your organization.

How to Get Meaningful Hands-on Skills

Many IT teams have a tough time getting on the radar screen of other functional departments that are looking for ways to leverage information and technology to drive their objectives. Now that organizations are talking about Digital Transformation as the latest path to drive performance and innovation, existing technology folks see more of the same. Fresh new faces are sitting in front of exciting new digital tools, and incumbents are chained to supporting legacy systems and stilted processes. Legacy systems are drab and unexciting, with a litany of limitations, exceptions, and manual workarounds, but still critical in the day-to-day operation of the as-is.

Your internal IT team will be a valuable addition to the Digital Transformation team; obviously, they will be much more in tune with legacy processes and existing culture. They will have the best grasp of the existing technology. But do they have the chops to take on tasks using newer ideas, platforms, and techniques in mobile, web, and cloud?

Building and maintaining skills in new technology can be difficult, but those skills can be critical in winning a seat at the table when the company is determining how to apply new ideas to their Digital Transformation. So how does IT break the cycle, and get the hands-on skills that are so important? Give yourself permission to think a little differently.

Physician, Heal Thyself

It is a common sentiment, a repeating pattern: we do not apply our talents and brilliance to our own efforts. Sure, a lot of it has to do

---

[22] Much like Xerox and White-Out, the brand name has become a verb.

with prioritization. You may be working on customers' requests and projects before your own, giving them a higher priority in the competition for your time. In a world where the customer is always right, this is a very common response.

But some of it has to do with our own fear of change. I am always fascinated by IT folks who resist change in how they do what they do. Engaged teams are constantly expecting their peers in other areas of the business to adapt to certain changes, like version upgrades for core systems, or increased controls and policies for cybersecurity. But when talk shifts to underlying tech topics like cloud vs. on-premise architectures – details that are typically out of sight from the end user – IT will often resist change to the investments they have already made in time, talent, and training.

The Cobbler's Children Have No Shoes

Alternatively, you may be falling into a selfless, customer-obsessed prioritization that prevents any and all self-improvement. You would be correct, for example, to treat your peer organizations like customers, focusing on service, the impact of change, and really being "obsessed" with understanding their needs and looking for solutions. But IT teams eventually get hit by an ever-increasing wave of requests; ask and you shall receive. The result is pretty consistent. The backlog of project and service requests grows quickly, and you cannot make time to learn new techniques, change core architecture, or improve your own internal process.

But the customer is *not* always right, especially when you expand the window of time impacted by a given decision or request. You could be incurring a load of technical debt every time you patch a broken process, implement a manual workaround, or just fall back on completely manual processes that could be effectively automated. The incremental cost of doing it the old-fashioned way may be low, but over time, this extra work adds up to a ton of time wasted – time that could be spent on more impactful work for your customers!

When you really think about it, IT may be acting inconsistently. Why do you suggest value from one direction (encouraging digital innovation for the business) as you walk down a completely different path (bypassing digital innovation for internal IT operations)? A much better approach would be to carve out a set portion of your time for process improvement and training. The short-term cost (time and expense) will always be offset by long-term savings – the time and expense that you can redirect toward impactful work for your internal customers, with faster time to value, less risk, and higher reliability.

Learn By Doing

Despite their fondest hopes, IT cannot match up critical internal needs with the kinds of new technology expertise that Marketing or Product Development desires. To be fair, if a given shiny object is bleeding edge, it may easily be too experimental to justify the time it might take to master it. But how does IT get hands-on experience with the close-to-cutting edge tech that can provide real value to your Digital Transformation?

A sure-fire way to win a seat at the table will be to have the hands-on skills – to be the ones who can write the dashboards, code the apps, architect and build the cloud, and even put together an effective machine learning model well enough to visualize how applicable it really can be.

How do you get these skills? Don't think so much – just do it! Train yourself by reading the documentation, watching the videos, and taking the online courses. It's not all rocket science. You will be amazed at how evolutionary most of this "new tech" really is.

How do you manufacture the time? Yes, it will not be a simple task to learn – if it were, everyone would be doing it. Schedule some time and make the commitment; you may have to mindfully sign yourself up for the nights-and-weekends work that it takes to learn.

What projects will you create and implement? That could be easy to determine – just look in the mirror. Start using new tech to work at problems that are stealing away time from your day. Make some improvements to the databases and spreadsheets that your teams use to manage projects, plan your work, model your resource constraints, or track and publish your performance metrics. Or build interfaces and aggregate information from your project tracker, your help desk ticketing system, and your financials and collaboration systems, to give your team and your internal business partners a dashboard that details how IT is delivering value.

What's in It for Me?

Remember, most companies will not want to build a new revenue stream using internal IT as their primary software development resource. That is typically not a core competency for traditional IT. But it is a great opportunity to learn new and exciting technical skills and concepts with a very understanding and patient customer – you!

When you are doing this for yourself and your team, you can safely demonstrate that initial lack of understanding, learn how to estimate and prioritize effort, and make all manner of embarrassing mistakes in front of a very understanding audience. When you make big mistakes, taking down production and requiring massive rewrites… well, the only ones experiencing the pain will be your own team. Some problems will occur, but at least you have a very understanding customer – yourself!

Who Should Own the Digital Transformation?

With all of these functional areas contributing to the goal, your organization will be in an excellent position to win. But who should lead the team? Put more plainly, who should drive the Digital Transformation of your business?

This question is being asked in many corporate leadership suites these days, and many departments (primarily IT and Marketing) assume that they have the clear claim to the title. In fact, we can easily make a case for Finance, Operations, or

Customer Service or even Corporate Communications (if such a role exists). It really doesn't matter which functional area this leader calls home, as long as the leader realizes that the role needs to understand a number of important concepts from the Five Components.

Product Management: This is a business, after all, and you will be expected to clearly describe the benefits and ROI. How will you quantify an ROI if your digital tactics are a big departure for the legacy business? You will need to identify directional metrics and design breakpoints in the process so you can iterate and hone your pitch into something that makes sense.

Process Design and Customer Service: Information without context is just noise; you'll need to understand and empathize with your customers and their world so you can deliver information that matters. And, you will want to seamlessly integrate with your legacy customer service processes for continuity and consistency.

Interaction Design that is appropriate for the target audience, and features compelling visuals with clear communication of function and value. This goes beyond the interface design for websites and apps. It's the holistic, information-based conversation you want to drive with your customers.

Solution Design and Development. More than just coding experience, it is important to have familiarity and comfort with concepts like data quality, process definition, and modern techniques like Continuous Development. Unlike cloud infrastructure, this area of digital delivery may be something that you choose to internalize if it is crucial to your plans.

Advanced Data Analytics and Artificial Intelligence. The Digital leader does not need to be a data scientist. But she should be able to clearly understand and articulate the capabilities and caveats of this core enabling technology, if only to be able to develop a coherent vision that is both transformative (truly differentiating) and sustainable (practical, conceivable, and achievable).

Project and Program Management are necessary to deliver integrated capabilities in a predictable, manageable manner. How will you balance agile, fast-twitch iterations with the eventual need to deliver a family of integrated services that are scalable and sustainable?

Interpersonal Communications. Digital Transformation will be new to your organization, and introduces a fundamentally different way to deliver value to the customer. If you are not comfortable with questioning the norm and changing peoples' closely held beliefs, you will struggle.

Which functional area of the business can do all of this? Obviously, no one is deep on everything listed here. The temptation might be to pick the two or three items with which you are most comfortable so that your Digital Strategy person will speak your language and the language of your organization. Alternatively, you might focus on areas where you are least comfortable. After all, if you had those skills, you would be doing it already!

The truth is, each skill is equally important, and none of them can be glossed over or underestimated. The ideal candidate will have experience and skills in all of those areas: deep experience for some, conversational experience in others. Enough to know, for example, when the IT team is overcomplicating the servers and pooh-poohing the cloud, or the Marketing group is struggling to build a meaningful business case, or the project is flailing, wasting time and money, from lack of a decent project manager.

The best Digital Leaders will have proven skills at leading cross-functional teams with demonstrated experience in all of those areas. Most of all, they must be able to effectively communicate vision and value to the project teams, the operations groups, the stakeholders, and your customers.

Chapter 11

Leading Change

There is a difference between *owning* your company's Digital Transformation and truly *leading* the change. Titles and organizational structures can show the outside world who may be responsible, but truly transformative change takes a different set of leadership skills beyond the standard requirements of business acumen (driving sustainable results), applied technology (translating the possible to the actual), and effective communications (connecting ideas to actions).

The successful change leader has a primary challenge: to find a link between these new "big ideas" and the current state of things.

Demonstrating the connection between the current state and the growth and improvement that change represents is a key to success. And what skills will be required? Think of the commonly used "people, process, and technology" mantra to put some structure to this. What types of change are we talking about?

- **People Change**: Soft skills and Emotional Intelligence[23] are typically required, but effective team leaders need to be able to command a room of strong personalities and competing agendas. Some leaders are direct, and can shout folks down and/or eloquently shift the group's understanding. Others work indirectly, creating understanding and acceptance in non-threatening, semi-private conversations.

- **Process Change**: It is easy to say "automate a mess, and you get an automated mess," but the challenges of process redesign are known to many. A certain amount of patience and insight is required to ferret out waste in the process, to understand and identify the critical elements and tasks, and to aggressively involve the eventual process owners, cementing their commitment for implementation by making them part of the design.

- **Technology Change**: Bright, shiny new technology is typically the preferred work area for those who want to make a real difference. But you need the ability to understand and implement new technologies quickly, in a sustainable and supportable fashion. Points are taken off for quickly implementing a fragile system.

The opportunity, of course, is to pick one or two of these areas and build your skills in making change happen. If you are not good in front of a group of people and are more comfortable working directly with the technology, focus on your change skills by understanding new developments and methods, and figuring out how to use them to make projects and processes happen faster with higher quality and more predictable outcomes. Looking for a stretch? Get into process design and development; it's not always about the bits and bytes, but systems thinking is a big plus, and process skills are often a great way to bridge from technology to people skills.

---

[23] Refers to the capability of an individual to recognize and manage their own emotions, and the emotions of others, and to handle interpersonal relationships empathetically.

Inspiration, Art, Science, and Execution

When trying to figure out how to make things happen, the focus switches between multiple targets. *"What am I doing? Why am I doing this? How can I get the others to understand what I am doing?"*

Real innovation happens along a continuum that stretches from The Big Idea to Real Results, and organizations that want to make real change and true innovation happen need to understand the different elements along the way.

Yes, I know – I just guided you to pick one or two specific areas (people, process, or technology), and develop your change managements skills there. Still true, but what about those who aspire to transformational leadership – who want to make innovation happen across the organization? A single person does not need to be expert in each of these areas, but leaders should actively work in all of them. Aspire to be a jack of all trades, a master of none. The ability to develop a vision, communicate it with impact, build something actionable, and follow through with the implementation are bankable skills that effective leaders need.

For each of these elements, think about their definitions, but also think of them in context with the other elements of the continuum. A leader with an impractical vision is just a dreamer; breakthrough science that is not well communicated will just sit on the shelf.

Inspiration

Defined: Inspiration is the ability to imagine what is possible. This does not have to be something as earth-shattering as the Internet or as imaginative as the iPad. Businesses are crying out for innovation in areas as mundane as cost controls, lean operations, and revenue growth. Make no small plans, and have the courage and the energy to stretch. Recognize the organization's practical limits, but do not sell them short. Your team might surprise you – and themselves.

In Context: There is a fine line between imagination and inspiration; we need something that can be implemented in our lifetimes. Flights of fancy can broaden your horizons, but you must eventually deliver real business results. This is where you can enable acceptance of the 80/20 rule – a practical vision that sees when enough is enough, that knows when to trim down the requirements to get 80 percent of the value with only 20 percent of the effort.

Art

Defined: Innovation often involves ideas, processes, or relationships that are difficult to understand simply because they involve remixing the as-is with something new. Sometimes innovation involves design and visualization – understanding a new structure, a changed process flow, or a hidden trend in the numbers. Sometimes it involves vocalization – an explanation or observation that needs just the right written or spoken words to trigger understanding and acceptance. And sometimes it involves insight and imagination – to come up with something that has never been done before.

In Context: As goods and services are commoditized, and descriptive data becomes freely available in deep detail, the value and importance of design continues to grow. Well-designed and executed words, pictures, sounds, thoughts, and ideas are the competitive differentiators that businesses need. Great leaders may possess acute verbal and/or visual communication skills, but do not discount the pizzazz required to make innovation happen in your organization. Invest time on a regular basis as you think about the design of things you see and hear every day. What images capture your eyes and your imagination? How do some documents convey meaning without boring you to tears?

Science

Defined. Sooner or later, you will have to create something that does not exist – a new product or service, a simplified process, an effective data visualization, or an impactful team. This will always involve some specific science – knowledge of an engineering discipline, a programming language, a commercial market, or a drawing tool. At some point, sustainable innovation must manifest itself as a repeatable, measurable process or event, and sooner or later, you will have to be able to translate your hand-waving into something that actually works.

In Context: Inspirational ideas need to find their way to the screen or the printed page so they can be communicated effectively, and communicated consistently. The best design ideas must make their way into the final product, moving from the top of your mind and the tip of your pencil to something that can be executed, like an app, a web service, a document or a project plan. The best leaders can still summon hands-on skills when needed; have you built something interesting in the past few months?

Execution

Defined: This is where the rubber meets the road. Results derive from making something happen. This could be the execution of a process, but can also refer to the coordinated steps in a project plan that implement a new product, or establishing rules, structure, and predictability where previously there was random action. Science has created something. Now it's time to get it implemented, and to make sure the promised results are delivered.

In Context: Starting a new process, stopping an old process, and bringing structure where there is disorder are the typical end results of most business projects. However, inertia and entropy are powerful natural forces, and blasting through resistance often relies on a strong idea that is communicated effectively and designed efficiently.

The toughest challenge for some entrepreneurs (and intrapreneurs!) is to know when to call for assistance. There is value in knowing everything about a single area, but sustainable success often comes to those who know when to call in the experts. The best business results scale across multiple people, teams, locations, business units, and processes. So why shouldn't the best leaders scale across multiple resources?

Never stop learning, never stop improving your skills in all of these areas, but know when to bring in the experts if you want to see results that surpass your expectations.

The Magic in the Middle

Now we move to the challenge of making this change happen. You must include the entire organization as you transform and change. But let's face facts; some will understand and embrace this new way of thinking and working, while others will not.

Consider the potential population for any new idea, process, product, or system. You can generalize everyone into three Pareto-inspired groups.

- **Top 20 percent**: These are the folks who "get it" and have the brains, the interest, and the desire to fully understand the new idea, process, product, or system. These people *will* gain the most benefit; in Pareto terms, they are the 20 percent that will receive 80 percent of the value.

- **Bottom 20 percent**: These are the "hopeless." They just don't get the concept, will need constant hand holding, have no interest in making any change to their norm, and have no desire to expand their horizons and learn something new. In Pareto terms, they are the 20 percent that cause 80 percent of the problems.

- **Middle 60 percent**: Simply put, this is everyone else. These are the folks who *could* derive value out of the idea, process, product or system, but need more hand holding, guided learning, and/or managerial promises to commit to learning how to use and apply the new ideas.

I call this last group "the magic in the middle" because these are the people you need to win over to ensure success for your Digital Transformation. Most projects would be considered a failure if they were only able to convince 20 percent of their target audience to make the change and realize the promised value. At the same time, no one expects 100 percent success, especially with the bottom 20 percent that will just never get it. So the make-or-break target market for training and retention is the middle 60 percent – the folks who need a reasonable level of vision, communication, documentation, training, and follow-up to get over the finish line.

Note that "magic" refers to a simple, but not necessarily intuitive, idea. What really differentiates success is the level of engagement for this make-or-break group, that middle region of 60 percent. It is not good enough that your top product managers understand the potential of digital products and services. The majority in the middle need a clear vision and practical examples, and require your attention and persistence to make the change. It is not good enough that your top engineers and data scientists understand the new methods and can catch early adopters. The bigger chunk of your team, with solid tech backgrounds but fewer change management and communication skills, need guidance to make sure these ideas can scale to fit the huge potential market out there.

Interesting Observation...

This is one of the core reasons why external comparisons are tough on traditional Marketing and Product Development teams. How many times have people in old-line businesses been asked for projects as flexible, ubiquitous, user-friendly, and high quality as Instagram, Amazon, and Gmail? Or tried to address internal communication and collaboration challenges with tools like Facebook, Twitter, and Slack? Why do folks look at highly funded, highly target-marketed sites or products and cynically wonder why their internal teams cannot turn over requests with the same level of speed and quality?

One key reason: those sites only need to go after the Top 5 percent of focused, engaged, and technically-able potential consumers. Why? Because the Internet is so big, and there is plenty of money to be made from such a small percentage of the total user population.

Unfortunately for most businesses, it is not sufficient to implement ideas, processes, and systems that are effective for only

20 percent of the target market. Expectations are higher, and 50 percent to 80 percent of the team or market needs to be reasonably engaged in a new process for the change to be judged effective.

Your teams must go after the "middle" group – the 60 percent of your target audience who need a lot more care and attention to understand and be effective in the ideas, processes, products, and systems you provide.

It's called "magic" for a reason. You can leverage a lot of value once you realize that the magic is in the middle.

Training: When you understand the low-end expectations for competence in your target audience, you can develop your training material at that level, and no lower.

Testing for 100 percent of all cases is exhausting and time consuming, and a real drain on resources. However, only testing the basics (the Top 20 percent) will not require a lot of rigor. Error checks are simplistic, and the level of scrutiny is much higher. If you want to do an acceptable amount of decent quality testing, your test cases should cover the use cases in the middle.

Vendors: Bringing them in for a demo? Salesmen typically target business scenarios that are the "low hanging fruit" (in the Top 20 percent), and it's easy to understand when we cannot handle the "worst case scenario" (the Bottom 20 percent). Get the sales team to demo something from a typical "day in the life for the Middle 60 percent." The Top 20 percent group is the easiest to service, and the Bottom 20 percent is the easiest to ignore. The magic is in the middle, and success here separates the excellent from the also-rans.

Knowing, Understanding, Empathizing

Do you *know* your job, or do you really *understand* your job? One difficult part of change is helping people to see the difference.

Of course, these are delicate conversations. You can't just walk in and ask people if they understand what they are doing. But how often have you had this conversation?

"I look at the TPS Report every morning, and I look for something that is negative in this column. If the layout of the report changes, I can't do my job; you are gonna have to rewrite this new version of the report."

What this person is really saying is: "I don't understand my job, I don't think on the job – I just respond to the stuff I am used to looking for."

The great unstated truth is that most folks do not understand what they do. They did not implement it, they inherited it. They know the *how*, but not the *why*. And human nature makes us avoid admitting our own ignorance.

As a result, resistance to change means resisting anything that upsets the As-Is. Unfortunately, the As-Is has a stealthy way of changing in little bits over time, and as folks who originated this particular process move on, taking their understanding with them. So starts the slow, steady spiral to complete irrelevance, and mindless adherence to non-value adding work.

Empathy Helps Overcome Entropy

To make change happen in these environments, it helps to have and demonstrate empathy for how people feel and think so you can lessen resistance and open minds.

Show your self-knowledge and humility by freely admitting when your understanding falls short. As a team member, speak up in public when you don't understand the underlying process. As a manager, encourage folks to raise their hands and ask for help. And please, make it easy for team members to seek help off-line, after the meeting ends, so they don't have to demonstrate their lack of understanding in public.

Realize, however, that there is a significant requirement to *get things done*; we do not have time to stop and deconstruct everything. There is significant business value in having a repeatable, lean process, and a protracted search for understanding is wasting daylight. Balance the importance of understanding with the need to get things done by designing, documenting, and implementing lean processes with incremental improvements that can drive results on day one, but can also mature and improve over time.

Set the expectation that understanding the job is just as important as doing the job, but do not forget that we are getting paid for our results, not our understanding.

Field Notes: Empathy Skills
for the Transformational Leader

Becoming a Digital Business is a journey that your entire organization will need to make. For the visionary leader, the anticipation for this journey can be both exciting and a little frustrating. *"Why won't the rest of the organization run to these great ideas?"*

Perhaps a little empathy is in order. When was the last time you embarked on a journey when you were not entirely sure of each step on the path?

I remember my first long-distance motorcycle ride. Over the course of the three-day ride, I found myself thinking about the parallels between this journey and going live on a new ERP system or similar digital change event. Both journeys included a range of feelings: excitement, frustration, self-doubt, tedium, second guessing, and dread.

Dread

As the date drew nearer, I was thinking an awful lot about the impending trip. I was not a long-time rider, having only started the prior year. When learning to ride, I was very aware that the process was made easier because I knew how to drive a car with manual transmission. But I was still not as smooth on my turns as the more experienced bikers I saw and talked with. And I had never done the long-haul cruise – managing luggage, memorizing routes, and watching the gas gauge.

I realized, of course, that my "dread" was more accurately described as a healthy respect of the unknown. I had spent a decent amount of time on the bike, including a few day-rides of reasonable distance. And the motorcycle riding community is terrific – easy to talk with and quick to share their experiences and help. But in the end, I'd never gone on a ride this long – 900 miles in three days – and I wasn't sure of what lay ahead. This lack of confidence was a noticeably new line of thinking for me.

Insight: When the go-live date for your ERP rollout approaches, most experienced implementers will express some healthy concern. They have seen all sorts of issues over the years; why should this one be any different? Deep down, however, they are actually quite calm; *"Been there, done that,"* they will think to themselves, and their prior experience will make the prospect of big change seem easy.

That is good for the tech team – but what about the people in the business going through the change? For most, this is their day-to-day, run-my-world, air-that-I-breathe system, and it's about to change, perhaps drastically. No amount of practice and training will 100 percent eliminate the healthy respect for the unknown.

Test

Of course, things did not go smoothly on my long distance adventure. I suffered a minor catastrophe on Day 1 (hint: turn off your lights when you park), starting an unfortunate chain of events that stemmed from a simple root cause. Hassles with my GPS device (issues that should have worked themselves out in test) caused these problems because I did not go on enough practice runs with the GPS connected. To be fair, I was still tinkering with the best way to mount the device on my bike. I had sporadic power issues for the rest of the weekend, but I also developed some configuration changes to address unanticipated issues that kept popping up.

Insight: Maybe it is hubris, or maybe the schedule is tight, but we always make trade-off decisions between time, features, and cost without fully understanding the risk. More system testing, at high load with non-digital people doing the testing, will always be a good investment. Conversely, when you make the decision to trim time off the testing cycle, be prepared for unexpected problems. And do not lose your cool when the inevitable occurs.

Support

The motorcycle riding community is terrific. I have asked tons of questions and received helpful answers, hints, and direction. On the road, riders acknowledge each other all the time. The variety of people you see on bikes – all ages and sizes – make it look very easy to navigate their big cruisers around the tightest parking lots. At times, it is both comforting and intimidating.

How do they make it look so easy? Why can't I make it look so easy? I know it's just a matter of time, practice, and experience. I can navigate parking lots in my car and coordinate complicated airline connections through foreign airports. No worries, done it a million times. But manage an 800-pound Harley? Call me Danny Duck Walk.

Insight: For the team going through a Digital Transformation project, the experienced project manager, techs, and analysts who know the new systems and processes so well can be both comforting and intimidating. The existing team members know their old systems and processes quite well – can't we just stick with what we know? And the learning curve looks so steep ... *I'll never get to be as good as The Experts ...*

Empathy

As I was riding along on a less eventful Day 2, my epiphany was all around the connections between my ride and the Digital Transformation projects I have been involved with (M&A, ERP, e-commerce, Big Data, Internet of Things, etc.) When you are enabling the innovation, driving the change, and leading the team, it helps to empathize with the people who are having change inflicted upon them. You are taking people out of their comfort zones, away from the systems, processes, and metrics that got them where they are today. You are taking them to places they haven't been, asking them to complete processes they have never done, and no amount of preparation will make all of their concerns go away.

You may not be able to remember the feelings of excitement, frustration, self-doubt, tedium, second guessing, and dread of your first big project because it is all second nature to you at this point. This lack of empathy will make you a less-than-effective leader and change agent.

So here is a bit of self-development advice. Find a personal "big change" project of your own, one that takes you well out of your comfort zone, and make it happen. Climb a mountain, learn a language, run a 10K, speak before a large audience. Push your comfort boundaries. Stretch your experience in ways you haven't before. Purposefully put yourself in a situation where you do not have any experience. Learn something new, and make it something that is a tad risky.

I think it is amazingly helpful to go through a big change, both personally and professionally. It can and should make you a more empathetic change leader. Getting people to accept and internalize transformational change is a critical part of the process. You may be able to come up with a brilliant strategic pivot, inspirational product re-imagining, foundational process redesign, or liberating system architecture. But if you cannot get people to change with you, you are just standing in a parking lot, waiting for a jump-start.

Field Notes: Conflict Is a Canary for Change

Are you intimidated by, or afraid of, conflict in your organization? Maybe it is just a signal that something else is going on.

What is the best response to conflict in the workplace?

What should the people on the team do?

What should a good leader do?

I had to address this once when issues began to surface with a working team. Folks were not tossing chairs around the room, but we had passive resistance, strong words in meetings, upset conversations, and private, formalized complaints. While listening to one particular thread of the discussion, an observation caught my attention – the idea that this conflict was going on during a time of great change.

Change was hitting the team from many directions, internally (as teams are built up and disbanded, and strategies and tactics come and go) and externally (as markets, customers, and channels shift and flow). Some compelling issues were hitting the proverbial fan.

Conflict from personalities and agendas, confusion and doubt, or creative energy and newfound flexibility seem to be a necessary part of the change process. And yet change can be an enabler of greatness, a purposeful intent, and a necessary response. So conflict, one might observe, can also be a good thing – an indicator that your change efforts are proceeding.

But what if you are not changing, yet conflicts seem to be popping up more than in the past? Maybe there is something going on that you are not aware of. Maybe conflict in your organization is actually a canary in your company's coal mine – an early indicator that change is imminent, necessary, or happening around you whether you want it or not.

By all means, manage the conflict in your team and your organization, but do not stifle it; there could be some interesting signals coming your way.

Chapter 12

Being Human in a Digital World

Does embarking upon a Digital Transformation still seem daunting to you? Do you doubt you can actually *do this?*

Do not doubt. The answer is yes, you can absolutely do this! We have looked at the theory, the strategy, and the deep thought behind a Digital Transformation, and simplified the steps to make them active and actionable. Remember that this type of thinking can be more evolutionary than revolutionary for your organization. Again, it will not be easy, but a simpler, clearer path that is aligned with the goals and strategy of your business, and the people within, will go a long way toward making your digital aspirations a reality.

Don't think so much about the height of the hills you are about to climb. Think more about the paths you will choose, the alternatives you will explore, and what you will learn on the overall journey. Recognize that success means different things to different teams. Make sure your journey is in line with the value creation that is at the core of your organization.

Change your Definition of Success

When most people talk about their work, success can be summarized with one simple word.

Done...

> *The lawn is mowed.*
>
> *The dishes are clean.*
>
> *The clothes are put away.*
>
> *I've read the book.*
>
> *I've written the book report.*

... seems to work for simple things around the house. What about work to be done around the job?

Done.

> *I've loaded the copier.*
>
> *I've scheduled the meeting.*
>
> *I've received the shipments.*
>
> *The books are closed.*
>
> *The ledger is balanced.*

But these are all tasks -- chunks of work with a neat, finite end point. What about non-tasks?

> *I've made my sales calls.*
>
> *I've documented the process.*
>
> *I've written the program.*
>
> *I've completed the spreadsheet.*
>
> *I've done the analysis.*

Done?

Are these really done? A better question might be to ask whether these are tasks that have ended, or whether they are part of a bigger objective.

> *I've made my sales calls...*
>
> > *now the orders will start coming in.*

I've documented the process...

> *now others will be able to do these tasks without me.*

I've written the program...

> *now it will perform as the user expects.*

I've completed the spreadsheet...

> *now others will be able to extend the model.*

I've done the analysis...

> *now it will correctly answer the questions we need answered.*

Does it really matter that you made the calls if they didn't get the sales? Not really; if you want to consider yourself a successful telesales rep, you will learn how you sound over the phone, adjust the message and the tone to put the caller at ease, do your homework before the call to have the background information ready, etc.

Does the documentation you produce matter if no one understands what you are saying? Not really. So you work on your style, and ask your readers for feedback: what is clear, what is not clear.

Does the spreadsheet add value if no one else can use it? Well, maybe you are just creating a tool to make your own life easier. But imagine if you could design a financial model that your peers could use to drive value? A rising tide lifts all boats...

Let's back the camera up even further to get a wider view of your Digital Transformation. Say you are rolling out a major new system, designing a comprehensive training program, implementing a new organization model, or developing a new product offering. Are you successful when the task is done? I do not think so.

Rolling out a major new system is successful only when people can use the system to great effect over the long term, and transfer that knowledge to new employees.

Designing a training system is successful only when people can learn about the new program, sign up for training when it fits in their schedules, take the courses, and apply the knowledge to create more value.

Implementing a new organizational model is successful only when people understand the new way of doing things, can make the transition, and then can sustain the new methods through the inevitable growing pains.

Developing a new product offering is successful only when you can generate sustainable, profitable new revenue, have connected with the customer to solve a valid need, and convinced them to actually pay for your products.

The definition of success is not simply completing tasks. A better definition focuses on results – quantifiable change, improved operations, smarter people, and more profitable top-line growth. There is a big difference between deliverables and results – and results are what the check signers are expecting.

Field Notes: Shades of Grey

Technology folks are, at times, not entirely comfortable with the world of business. Especially for those just out of school, there seem to be "shades of grey" that mysteriously guide the thinking and actions of leaders and teams. How can I reconcile this with the binary, black-and-white world of digital?

My undergraduate degree is in Electrical Engineering (EE). With all of my electives in chips, wires, and systems programming, today it would be called Computer Engineering. The passage of time has not changed much of this core technology. Modern systems architecture may have a few added layers of abstraction, but there isn't much difference from the lessons of those courses, with the fundamental concept of the binary switch (On! Off!) representing a single "bit" of information at the heart and soul of the computer.

Since it was an EE degree, I had to take my fair share of courses on electronics and circuits – the bones and blood vessels of a typical computer. In second semester Circuits, we learned about the foundational electronic component of the modern era – the transistor, that magical three-lead device that we use to represent this fundamental on-off switch.

In one particular session, the professor was at the board drawing a wave form of the voltage across the two leads of the transistor. "When the voltage here moves up to 1.0 volts, we say the 'switch' is in the 'on' state (True, 1, Yes). And, when we change the inputs and the voltage is set to 0.0 volts, we say the 'switch' is in the 'off' state (False, 0, No)."

"However," my professor continued, "this is, after all, a physical device, and your designs have to account for certain material variations and losses across the device. So strictly speaking, we say that any voltage from 0.7 to 1.0 can be considered 'on' (True, 1, Yes). And, any voltage value from 0.0 to 0.3 can be considered 'off' (False, 0, No)."

Now, when most people retell stories from the past, they always get better as time goes by. But this is full disclosure: I clearly remember that I was the smart aleck in the room. I dutifully raised my hand to ask, "What if the voltage is 0.4 or 0.5?"

"Well," the professor demurred, "then you have an 'indeterminate state' – neither 1 nor 0, on or off – and that is a problem in your circuit. It is up to the circuit designer to make sure the input values have enough power to get a clean reading of the state of the switch."

I sat back in my chair and contemplated this great insight. Even the digital computer, that bastion of black-and-white certainty, must deal with shades of grey.

Don't Think So Much

There are many lessons to learn from that last story. Some might despair at the inability to impose order on a chaotic world. At the heart of it, digital is bound to fail due to the inexorable forces of entropy[24].

I prefer to take a different lesson: to accept the shades of grey as a given, and embrace the discoveries and setbacks as necessary steps along the journey. The journey exists to get us to the end, or more practically, to the end of the current big change initiative. Hopefully, we can complete it before the next big change comes along!

So do not get too caught up looking for a comprehensive answer and the perfect plan to get there. Don't think so much about the details. It may paralyze your team and your organization, and effectively block your company from creating the value.

Use the frameworks in this book to put a simple structure on your transformative change. Find a clear way to describe the objective, the strategy, and the first few steps to get there. Connect with other practitioners to test your thinking, focus your efforts, educate your teams.

And try to maintain a sense of humanity about things. Remember, a Digital Business will only succeed when it understands how to connect with *people*. And your Digital Transformation will only succeed when it incorporates ideas like human-centered design, tech- and soft-skills development, and a real focus on engagement and inclusion with the people in your company who will interact with these digital tools to get the work done.

Digital Business can create real value for all stakeholders – employees, customers, suppliers, shareholders – as long as the human factor of these relationships is kept in mind.

---

[24] The universe's central oxymoron – 'change is constant'

References

Clarke, Arthur C. 1973. *Profiles of the Future: An Inquiry into the Limits of the Possible.* Madison, Wisconsin USA: Harper & Row.

Collis, David, and Michael G. Rukstad. 2008. "Can You Say What Your Strategy Is?" *Harvard Business Review*, April.

Edmans, Alex. 2016. "28 Years of Stock Market Data Shows a Link Between Employee Satisfaction and Long-Term Value." *Havard Business Review.* 24 March. https://hbr.org/2016/03/28-years-of-stock-market-data-shows-a-link-between-employee-satisfaction-and-long-term-value

Fry, Richard. 2018. "Millenials are the largest generation in the U.S. labor force." *Pew Research Center.* 11 April. https://www.pewresearch.org/fact-tank/2018/04/11/millenials-largest-generation-us-labor-force/

Garrad, Lewis, and Tomas Chamarro-Premuzic. 2016. "The Dark
    Side of High Employee Engagement." *Harvard Business
    Review.* 16 April. https://hbr.org/2016/08/the-dark-
    side-of-high-employee-engagement

MacLennan, James P. 2014. "A Framework for Starting the
    Internet of Things Conversation." *Maker Turtle.* 17
    September. https://www.makerturtle.com/a-framework-
    for-starting-the-internet-of-things-conversation/

—. 2016. "IoT Field Notes: How to Identify Customer Value."
    Maker Turtle. 10 April. https://www.makerturtle.com/iot-
    field-notes-how-to-identify-customer-value-2/

—. 2014. "The Digital Project Budget: How Much?" *Maker Turtle.*
    10 November. https://www.makerturtle.com/the-digital-
    project-budget-how-much/

—. 2016. "The Five Core Components of a Great Digital
    Business." *Maker Turtle.* 20 November.
    https://www.makerturtle.com/the-five-core-components-
    of-a-great-digital-strategy/

—. 2006. "The Law of Large Numbers - or, why Enterprise Wikis
    are Fundamentally Challenged." *Maker Turtle.* 26
    September. https://www.makerturtle.com/the-law-of-
    large-numbers-or-why-enterprise-wikis-are-
    fundamentally-challenged/

Porter, Michael E. 2001. "Strategy and the Internet." *Harvard
    Business Review*, March.

Porter, Michael E., and James E. Heppelmann. 2014. "How
    Smart, Connected Products are Transforming
    Competition." *Harvard Business Review*, November.

Porter, Michael E., and Victor E. Millar. 1985. "How Information
    Gives You Competitive Advantage." *Harvard Business
    Review*, July.

Ries, Eric. 2011. *The Lean Startup: How Today's Entrepreneurs
    Use Continuous Innovation to Create Radically Successful
    Businesses.* Currency.

Sinek, Simon. 2011. *Start with Why: How Great Leaders Inspire Everyone to Take Action.* Portfolio.

Tufte, Edward. n.d. *The Work of Edward Tufte and Graphics Press.* https://www.edwardtufte.com

Index

- W -

About the Author

James P. MacLennan is the Chief Information Officer at IDEX Corporation, a diversified industrial manufacturer that sells highly engineered products to customers in a variety of markets worldwide.

Prior to IDEX, Jim held leadership roles at Pactiv LLC and Reynolds Consumer Products, Culligan International, Searle Pharmaceuticals (Monsanto), and other diverse organizations.

Jim has broad experience in a variety of business models and markets, translating strategic drivers into tactical plans and tangible results. His career spans multiple industries, including real estate / property management, building construction and maintenance services, pharmaceuticals, consumer durables, industrial manufacturing, and consumer package goods. He started his career at a software development and consulting firm, which gives him a unique insight to the role of Digital in creating value, and the power of great teams to bring that promise to life.

Jim has a Bachelor of Science degree in Electrical Engineering from the University of Notre Dame, and an MBA in Marketing from DePaul University. He regularly publishes his observations and insights at www.makerturtle.com.

Made in the USA
Monee, IL
31 October 2020